ALTERNATIVES: THE UNITED STATES CONFRONTS THE WORLD

Fernand Braudel Center Series
Edited by Immanuel Wallerstein

Alternatives: The United States Confronts the World
by Immanuel Wallerstein

The Modern World-System in the Longue Durée
edited by Immanuel Wallerstein

*Overcoming the "Two Cultures": Science vs. the Humanities
in the Modern World-System*
Richard E. Lee and Immanuel Wallerstein, coordinators

ALTERNATIVES: THE UNITED STATES CONFRONTS THE WORLD

IMMANUEL WALLERSTEIN

Paradigm Publishers

BOULDER • LONDON

Copyright © 2004 by Paradigm Publishers

Published in the United States by Paradigm Publishers, 3360 Mitchell Lane, Suite C, Boulder, Colorado 80301 USA.

Paradigm Publishers is the trade name of Birkenkamp & Company, LLC, Dean Birkenkamp, President and Publisher.

Library of Congress Cataloging-in-Publication Data has been applied for.

Printed and bound in the United States of America on acid-free paper that meets the standards of the American National Standard for Permanence of Paper for Printed Library Materials.

Designed and Typeset by Straight Creek Bookmakers.

09 08 07 06 05 04
5 4 3 2 1
ISBN 1-59451-066-0 (cloth)
ISBN 1-59451-067-9 (paper).

Contents

To the Reader

Since 1998, I have been publishing on the web commentaries on the state of the world (http://fbc.binghamton.edu/commentr.htm). On the website is a note that reads: "These commentaries, published twice monthly, are intended to be reflections on the contemporary world scene, as seen from the perspective not of the immediate headlines but of the long term." This book, in its middle part, reproduces some of these commentaries. But the whole book is meant to be a reflection on the contemporary world scene from the perspective of the long term.

I believe that the United States has been wrestling for over thirty years with the problem of its relative decline in the world-system. George W. Bush's "war on terrorism" marks a distinctive turning point in U.S. world policy, a break with the strategies (if not with the underlying policies) pursued by all previous presidents since Richard Nixon. As you will see, I believe that, in trying to change things in a direction that would restore the world power of the United States, Bush has actually weakened the United States still more. And furthermore, he has made it impossible to return to the previous strategy, a strategy that I call "soft multilateralism."

The question before the United States today is not whether we should be multilateralist (in the sense this term has been used by previous presidents) or unilateralist (as Bush's critics correctly suggest he is). It is whether we can devise a quite new policy that is far more realistic and far more progressive than the previous one, following neither the Bush strategy nor that of the previous thirty years. It will not be easy—either to change the policy or to have it make a real difference in the world-system. But if the United States does not make a basic turnaround in the way it relates to the world, the consequences will be disastrous, first of all for the United States but also for the rest of the world.

Immanuel Wallerstein
February 15, 2004

Part I

Terrorism: The Bush Fiasco

The greatest threat to the United States today—its liberty, its security, its prosperity, its future—is the United States. For at least thirty years, the United States had already been wandering uncertainly and hesitatingly down a slippery incline, when George W. Bush decided to rush full speed ahead. As a result, the U.S. is in immediate danger of falling badly, perhaps fracturing itself. After the dramatic and terrible September 11 attack on the United States, Bush listened to his covey of hawks, and declared a "war on terrorism"—one in which he told the whole world that it was either "with us or against us" and one, he said, that the United States would "surely win." This bravura was the public face of just about the worst strategy the U.S. government could have adopted, not only weakening the United States and the world considerably in the subsequent years but also strengthening all those forces it was ostensibly designed to destroy.

How did the United States come to place itself in such a disastrous position? It was surely not inevitable. The hawks around George W. Bush were determined to transform the world, and they have, but not at all in the way they hoped. The basic premise of the Bush hawks was that the U.S. had been in a slow decline for at least thirty years—which is true. In their analysis, however, this decline was the result of a weak and faulty policy of successive presidents, therefore reversible. All the U.S. needed to do, they argued, was to flex seriously its considerable military muscle, abandon all pretense of multilateral consultation with hesitant and weak allies, and proceed to intimidate both dubious friends and hostile enemies alike, and the U.S. would be in the world driver's seat again. This, however, was not at all true.

The U.S. decline is structural, the result of the predictable loss of the enormous economic edge the United States temporarily had after 1945 vis-à-vis everyone, including all the other so-called industrialized countries. In a capitalist system, such an edge—especially the outsized advantage the U.S. had in the 1950s and 1960s—is impossible to maintain, since others can and will copy the technology and organization that make it momentarily possible. This is exactly what happened. By circa-1970, Western Europe and Japan had brought their economic structures to the point where they were more or less competitive with the U.S. structures—in their home markets, in the home market of the United States, and in the markets of the rest of the world. The decline from the giddy but passing economic dominance and therefore hegemony in the world-system that the U.S. experienced is something one lives with, adjusts to, and makes the best of. The decline of an erstwhile hegemonic power is really less about its own decline than about the rise of the others. Thus its decline is initially only relative (it commands an ever-smaller proportion of world value produced and capital accumulated). And the decline can be slow. But it is not something that can be reversed in any fundamental way. Once the hegemonic peak has been reached and then passed, it cannot be regained. Trying to restore the glorious past only hastens the pace of the decline.

The hawks do not see it that way. They have the vision of an imperial America always on top, always impregnable, virtually by moral right. They believe that supremacy in the economic and political arenas can be imposed and reimposed *manu militari*. The position of the hawks has been so egregiously arrogant that they could not get their way for a long time. Quite the contrary. Instead, in the thirty years after 1970, from Nixon to Carter to Reagan to Clinton, the U.S. government did its best to deal with an increasingly difficult situation with the strategy that I call "soft multilateralism."

The primary object of this strategy was to slow down as much as possible the process of decline of U.S. primacy in the world that had resulted from the loss of the once-unquestioned supremacy of the United States in industrial production. The three main pillars of this Nixon-to-Clinton strategy were (1) *partnership:* the attempt to keep our allies from striking off on independent political (and military) paths by emphasizing past politico-moral debts and continuing common enemies, and offering them a right of prior consultation on new initiatives in their role as "partners"; (2) *nuclear oligopoly:* maintenance of the status quo in the list of nuclear powers by persuading and/or intimidating middle powers (especially Third World countries) to avoid pursuing any and all roads to nuclear proliferation; and (3) *globalization:*

the reorganization of world economic macrostructures by persuading and pressuring countries of the South— the peripheral zones located primarily in Asia, Africa, and Latin America—to renounce protectionist, developmentalist policies in favor of opening their economic frontiers, especially their financial borders. I call these policies *soft* multilateralism because the U.S. was always ready to go unilateral if it thought it had to. It simply did not say so out loud, in the hope that going it alone would not be necessary. The United States counted on its ability to "lead"—that is, to persuade others to endorse the decisions that the U.S. favored and which best served U.S. interests.

What one can say about this Nixon-to-Clinton strategy, pursued over thirty years, is that it was partially successful, in that the decline of the U.S. was indeed slowed down, but of course never reversed. The neo-cons, however, saw the glass as half-empty rather than half-full. They therefore proposed to improve the score in the pursuit of the same three objectives by using a new, tougher line. For a long time, their views were considered adventurous and outside the mainstream. And they were very frustrated, even with the Reagan administration. The attack of September 11, however, gave them at last the excuse they needed to implement their program, which had been advertised in advance in the 2000 report issued by the Program for a New American Century. Indeed, they had promoted an invasion of Iraq unceasingly since 1997. After 9/11, they went into high gear and the regime in power was ready to move forward. When, eighteen months later, U.S. troops entered Baghdad, they celebrated wildly. Now, they thought, all good things would follow. This program, imposed on the U.S. Congress and public in general through deception, manipulation, and demagoguery, has in fact been disastrous—above all, for the United States, which is far weaker today on the world scene than it was before September 11.

The hawks expected that the war in Iraq would be easily consummated. It has proved to be slow and draining, a continuing bleeding of lives and money with no immediate prospect of closure. The hawks expected that the traditional U.S. allies would respond to the display of military strength and determination by abandoning their hesitant steps toward political independence. Today, instead, the Paris-Berlin-Moscow axis, only a remote possibility in 2000, has become a continually developing reality with which Washington must deal. For the first time in history, Canada was not willing to participate in a war fought by its two closest allies, the United States and Great Britain. Today, the U.S.'s once-firm allies in East Asia—Japan and South Korea—are dragging their feet about sending troops to Iraq to help out the U.S. because public opinion at home is so hostile to the idea, and both countries have insisted that the troops they did send would not be engaged in combat operations. The hawks expected that, once Iraq has been divested of weapons of mass destruction, others like Iran and North Korea would abandon their pretensions to nuclear weaponry. But the U.S. found no weapons of mass destruction in Iraq, and both North Korea and Iran have clearly speeded up rather than slowed down their programs of obtaining a nuclear arsenal, even as they make not too meaningful gestures about inspections. And the U.S. finds that it can't really do very much about it.

The true lesson of the invasion of Iraq concerns the *limitations* of the huge military power of the United States. Of course, today, the U.S. is far ahead of any other country—and, certainly, of a weak country like Iraq—in military strength. Of course, the U.S. is able to win battlefield operations. And, up to a point, it can deal with the threat of covert operations by nonstate hostile groups, although this requires constant expensive vigilance and an appreciation that the ability to prevent such attacks will always be less than perfect. Some of them will succeed.

But in the end one has to be able to control the situation politically. War, as Clausewitz reminded us, is only the continuation of politics by other means. It is not a substitute for politics. Military prowess is hollow without political strength. And politically, the United States is weaker, not stronger, as a result of the Iraq war. Let us analyze this zone by zone.

Let us start with Europe. Ever since 1945, the alliance with Europe, Western Europe, was supposed to be the Rock of Gibraltar on which U.S. foreign policy was based. Europe, it was said, shared U.S. values. The dominant groups in the United States were all of European extraction. The cultural ties were deep. And of course, there were all kinds of institutional ties—military (NATO), economic (first the Marshall Plan, later OECD), political (G-7, the Trilateral Commission). If there were quarrels from time to time (particularly with France), these were in the end minor. When the chips were down, Western Europe and the U.S. were believed by both to be on the same side—as the joint bearers of the Judeo-Christian legacy, as the heirs of Greece and Rome, as the Free World versus the Communist world, as the North versus the South. All this was in fact largely true.

Relations now, however, have become quite frayed. No doubt, lip service is still being paid to the alliance, but the seeds of distrust are deep. The neo-cons basically scorn contemporary Europe, and have spread their views to a much larger U.S. public. They see Europeans as too pacifist (even cowardly), too addicted to the welfare state, too ready to appease the Muslim world, too "old-fashioned" (recall Rumsfeld's famous characterization of those less enthusiastic toward the U.S.'s Iraq policies as the "old Europe"). That many American people have felt this way about Europe is nothing new. What is new is that the view became official policy.

What this public proclamation of disdain did was trigger a European response that will not be easy to overcome. Many journalists speak in a facile manner about rampant "anti-Americanism" in Europe, especially in France. This is a gross exaggeration and, in many respects, actually less true of France than of other parts of Europe. But to frame the discussion in this way is to miss the cultural reality. Until 1945, Europe was in cultural terms the parent, or at least the elder sibling, of the United States, and this was the view not only of Europeans but of Americans themselves. Europeans tended to think of Americans as cultural adolescents, rebellious but naive. The Second World War changed all that. The United States emerged as the world's hegemonic power, the economic powerhouse, the political protector of Western Europe against the Soviet Union, and in cultural terms the new center of Western, indeed of world, culture.

In the thirty or so years of American hegemony after 1945, the United States learned to hone its cultural rough edges; it tried to cease being Graham Greene's "ugly American." And Europeans learned to accept, even admire, the United States—for its technology, to be sure, but even for its political philosophy. Still, even among the most pro-American of Europeans, the switch in relative cultural status rankled. As European economic self-confidence rose again, and as Europe began to construct itself politically, there commenced a strong drive to reassert an autonomous, powerful cultural presence in the world that would be distinctively European. Thanks to Bush, this drive, so natural and so evident, has now come to be defined as one that should and will distinguish itself very clearly from the United States—culturally, and therefore politically as well as economically. Europe and the United States are now going their separate ways. They are not enemies, but the days of automatic alliance—at any level—are forever over.

The story of Russia is different. The collapse of the Soviet Union, though considered a positive thing by many, perhaps even most, Russian citizens, represented nonetheless a striking downgrading of Russian power in the world-system. This was most particularly evident in the military arena. As a consequence, Russia not only had to restructure itself internally, with all the difficulties that entailed, but also had to reposition itself on the world scene. The 1990s, the Yeltsin decade, is not one on which Russians look back with enthusiasm. During this period, Russia suffered a lowering of its standard of living, severe internal polarization, the financial crisis of 1997, the crumbling of its military strength and morale, and internal threats to the unity of the residual Russian federation (most notably the continuing war in Chechnya).

When Putin came to power in 2000, his program was clearly the restoration not only of internal order and economic growth within Russia but of Russian power in the world-system. The question was how to do it, and in particular what diplomatic stance to take. Putin obviously did not want to recreate a cold war antagonism toward the United States. He flew to Crawford, Texas, to make a deal with George W. Bush. What he wanted most of all was to be accepted by the U.S. once again as a major player on the world scene. But behind all the flowery language, equality on the world scene was the one thing Bush was not ready to concede to Russia. So Putin began to play the field, seeking better relations in all directions—Western Europe (particularly Germany), China, India. And of course, he wished to reassert a central role for Russia in the Middle East, a continuing priority of Russian foreign policy since at least the eighteenth century.

The Iraq war was a decisive moment, crystallizing the results of three years of tentative outreach. For what Bush did, in effect, was to tell Russia that the U.S. did not consider it a major player even in the Middle East (and therefore, implicitly, not anywhere). Indeed, the United States used the occasion of the Iraq war to create and/or deepen the U.S.'s ties with countries formerly part of the Soviet Union—Central Asian countries in particular, but also Georgia and Azerbaijan. Far from reaffirming Russia's role, the U.S. was in fact working further to diminish it. France and Germany on the other hand reached out to Russia—as a permanent member of the Security Council, but also, no doubt, as a counterweight to the pro-American tendencies of the east-central European countries.

What had always been a theoretical possibility—a Paris-Berlin-Moscow axis—was stimulated into existence by the unilateralist pretensions of the Bush regime. The difficult initial building-blocks of this alliance were put into place by George W. Bush. The rest of the construction will be done by the three countries. As with all such structures, once consolidated, it will be hard to tear down. The world has passed from a theoretical possibility to a practical process.

As for the Muslim world, it has been a problem for the United States for all of the last half-century. This is the case for two reasons: the active and ever-greater commitment of the United States to Israel—not merely to its right to exist but to its ongoing policies vis-à-vis the Palestinians and the Arab world in general; and the continuing active intervention of the United States in the region because of the importance of its oil deposits. Bush did not create these tensions. What he has done is worse. He has undone the basic mechanism by which the U.S. government and most regimes in the region had hitherto managed to keep the tensions under some control. This mechanism was U.S. collusion in the deliberate ambiguity of the governments of the region in their public stance vis-à-vis the United States. In practice, they did most of what the United States wanted them to do (including at the military level) while frequently employing a quite different public rhetoric and, most important, allowing the multiple movements hostile to the United States (now grouped under the loose label of "terrorist" movements) to continue to work and even flourish within their borders.

The game of ambiguity was a constantly dangerous one for the regimes, as Anwar Sadat learned to his peril. The governments had to be very careful not to tilt too far in one direction or the other. But on the whole it was a possible game to play, and it satisfied the needs of the United States. Two regimes in particular were crucial in this regard: Saudi Arabia and Pakistan. It is therefore no accident that Osama bin Laden made it clear that the actions of his group, and most notably the September 11 attack, had as its primary objective the bringing down of these two regimes. What he hoped would happen, and it obviously did, was that the United States would react by insisting that these regimes end their ambiguity in the light of 9/11. It called upon them to throw themselves publicly and fully into the "war against terrorism." The U.S. largely succeeded with Pakistan, but thus far only partially with Saudi Arabia. The problem is that, once the veil of ambiguity is torn asunder, it cannot be easily restored. We shall see if the two regimes can survive. Any replacement regimes will be far less friendly to the United States.

At the same time, the hawks in Israel have taken advantage of the unprecedented level of support they have gotten from the Bush regime to destroy the Palestinian Authority, which had also been playing the same game of ambiguity. The Oslo accords may never have achieved their objective of an agreed-upon two-state outcome, but the real point here is that the world cannot go back to anything like the Oslo accords. It has been said for the last thirty years that only the United States could mediate the Israeli-Palestinian dispute. It seems to me that what Bush has done is to achieve the exact opposite. The United States is now totally compromised, and if there is ever to be a political resolution of the dispute, which seems increasingly unlikely, it will come about only if the United States is *not* involved in the process.

Latin America has been considered by the United States to be the latter's backyard, its private hunting-ground and zone of prime influence. The Monroe Doctrine dates, after all, from 1823. The Latin American revolutionary wave of the 1960s, which challenged U.S. dominance, was brought in check by the mid-1970s. As of 2000, the U.S. government could feel relatively relaxed about the political evolution of the continent. The governments were in civilian hands, the economic frontiers were largely open, and, except for Cuba, no government was hostile.

By 2004, the tone of the continent had radically changed. There are two reasons for this. On the one hand, the Bush regime overplayed the U.S. hand by deciding to push full steam ahead with the proposed Free Trade Area of the Americas (FTAA) at the very moment that Latin American governments found themselves in great economic difficulties as a result of the 2000–2003 recession. In particular, there was the spectacular crash of Argentina, the poster-child of the International Monetary Fund (IMF) of the 1990s. This crash affected not merely the working classes but the middle classes as well, who massively lost their savings and saw their standard of living collapse. The net outcome of three years of changing governments, popular insurrections, and general turmoil was a populist government that openly thumbed its nose at the IMF and has gotten away with it, to the great applause of the Argentinean people.

There have been parallel leftward thrusts elsewhere in Latin America with varying degrees of strength. In Brazil, economically the most important country, the Partido dos Trabalhadores (Workers Party), under Lula, won the elections. And while Brazil is not (yet) thumbing its nose at the IMF (to the dismay of many of Brazil's intellectuals), it is leading the struggle against the FTAA and acquiring support in this action from governments across the continent that had been expected to react more conservatively. Indeed, Brazil's brilliant diplomatic effort is moving Latin America toward a collective autonomy it has never known before.

If this has been possible, and this is the second reason for the change in atmosphere, it is because the United States has been so overwhelmed with its concentration on and difficulties in Iraq and the Middle East in general that it has been unable to expend the effort it traditionally did to hold Latin American resistance in check. This not only accounts for its surprisingly vacillating policy in Venezuela but also explains why it could not persuade either Mexico or Chile, among the Latin American governments most friendly toward the U.S., to support it in its quest for a Security Council resolution on Iraq in February 2003.

Are there not any bright spots? The Bush regime thinks it can point to three: east-central Europe, India, and Israel. In general, the countries of east-central Europe have had deeply pro-American policies ever since the collapse of the communisms and of the Soviet Union. The United States represented for them protection against the possible resuscitation of both Communism and Russia as an imperialist state as well as the nirvana of consumer wealth. They were not at all attuned to the West European need to separate themselves culturally and politically from the United States. Quite the contrary. Such sentiments of course predate George W. Bush and, indeed, had already begun to wane in the last years of Clinton. What Bush has done is to seize the opportunity of the so-called war on terrorism to pursue an active campaign of establishing military bases and other forms of active political cooperation in this region as well as in former Soviet republics in Central Asia and the Caucasus.

So, as the West European and the Russian reaction to these American intrusions takes concrete form, it is forcing choices on the east-central European countries that they would happily avoid. The situation is similar to the United States' forcing the end of ambiguity in the Muslim world. It amounts to a lose-lose option for the countries involved. And in the long run, Western Europe and Russia have more leverage than the United States, since the U.S. cannot supply the kind of economic assistance demanded by the populations of these countries. Nor is the U.S. ready to treat east-central Europe to the same relaxed visa arrangements it offers Western Europe, which is bitter news for these governments. Therefore, even in what seems to be the sunny climes of east-central Europe and Central Asia, the United States has set itself up for a fall that, when it occurs, will smash the possibility of the slow development of relations on which previous U.S. regimes had built their hopes and strategies.

India is a similar case in point. The basis of an improved relationship between India and the United States has been India's hope and expectation, first, that the U.S. would reverse its historic tilt toward Pakistan and, second, that the U.S. would give India a sizable slice of the technological pie because of the latter's vast supply of skilled personnel in the most profitable sectors of the world-economy. But, as in east-central Europe and Central Asia, the United States, by implicitly overpromising, has set itself up for a fall. For India is, in the medium run, a competitor in informatics and pharmaceutics and not an ally. And the U.S. cannot afford to loosen its ties with Pakistan. Quite the contrary. Its headache is that Pakistan might decide to loosen its ties with the United States. In any case, India is now responding to Brazilian seduction to create a Third World economic alliance.

As for Israel, the Bush administration has tied itself so closely to the fate of the Sharon/Likud regime that it risks going under when the regime does. And this is just a matter of time. The U.S. has shed the last vestige of any pretense toward being the neutral mediator. It will thereby find itself squeezed out of the equation.

There remains one last zone, East Asia—in many respects the most crucial for the future of the United States. And here, too, the Bush regime has shown itself to be most imprudent, although perhaps a bit more wary and cautious than in other regions. China is holding a very strong hand. It is a powerhouse of industrial growth. It is steadily gaining military strength. And it is conducting a foreign policy designed to create strong ties in East and Southeast Asia. Given the Bush economic policy at home, which has led to a massive and ever-growing deficit and imbalance of trade, the United States finds itself more dependent on China than the other way around. It needs continued Chinese purchase of U.S. Treasury bonds. And while there are good reasons for China to do this in its own interests, the policy is one that has negative implications for China and, in any case, is not the only possible one. So the U.S. finds itself unable to take a tough line with China on anything really important. Meanwhile, Japan is making an economic comeback. And the two Koreas are moving very slowly, but somewhat ineluctably, toward closer ties, perhaps even reunification.

Ten years from now it will be clear that what Bush has hastened is the creation of an East Asian zone of entente and, therefore, a powerful limit to U.S. power and authority in this region of the world. It is not that East Asia will necessarily be hostile to the United States. Rather, Bush has ensured that the future geopolitical and geoeconomic alliance of East Asia and the United States, faced with a resurgent Europe (which includes Russia), will be arranged more on East Asian terms than on U.S. terms.

As the United States loses manufacturing and white-collar jobs (especially in information technology and even biotechnology) to East Asia and Europe, it will seek to hold on to its one remaining strength, which is in the financial arena. And here the dollar is crucial. The dollar has gone up and down vis-à-vis other strong currencies for the last fifty years, but this has been largely the United States' doing. The strength of the dollar has always been a function not of its exchange rate but of the fact that it has been the only reserve currency in the world since

1945. And the reason for this has been not U.S. economic strength but U.S. political strength. Governments and capitalists across the world have felt safest holding dollars. And they have been correct in making this judgment until now.

The crazy economic policies of the Bush regime are bringing this political strength to an end. Given the incredible deficits that the Bush regime has been accumulating (and they are threatening to go much higher), governments and capitalists are no longer certain that the safe place to hold their money is in dollars. And of course, objectively, they are wise not to be certain. It is a matter of political and economic judgment and psychological comfort. This process is one that suddenly tilts and, once tilted, will not right itself. We can expect that this tilt will occur within the next few years. It is hard to see how it can be stopped now. After that, there will be no safe currency, with all the implications this has for economic chaos. But geopolitically, this circumstance will remove the last, surest lever with which the United States has been able to put pressure on other countries.

None of the foregoing was, as I have said, inevitable. The trends were always there, but they were unfolding slowly. What might have taken thirty years to come to pass, Bush has ensured will occur in five or ten. And instead of the soft landing that might have been possible, the United States is in for a very hard landing. The question now is not how this situation can be reversed— it no longer can—but what would be an intelligent way to handle the very rough waters through which the ship of state is passing. Part II of this book will review the Bush fiasco as it unfolded between 2001 and 2004. Part III will offer a possible alternative mode through which the United States might relate to the rest of the world in the next thirty to fifty years.

Part II

Bush Encounters the World: Commentaries, 2001–2004

January 15, 2001: *"The World and George W. Bush"*

George W. Bush is the first U.S. president of the twenty-first century, and the world is nervous. Outside the United States, everyone is discovering how much they appreciated Bill Clinton. He turned out to be a far better U.S. president from their point of view than they had ever expected. This was not at all because they agreed with Clinton's policies all of the time, or even most of the time. It is because the world found him intelligent, well-informed, a good listener, and, above all, the best variety of U.S. president they could reasonably expect, given U.S. power, arrogance, and self-centeredness—what the French would call a *pis-aller*.

The rest of the world by and large hoped (and expected) that Al Gore would succeed Clinton and carry on. They are surprised (and dismayed) by the actual results. The world fears, rightly, that George W. Bush has none of the particular qualities Clinton displayed, and that the power, arrogance, and self-centeredness will be all that's there. I earlier suggested that there is little basic difference in the foreign policy conducted by Bush than would have been the case had Gore become president. But this equivalence needs to be qualified.

When it is said in the United States that there exists a "bipartisan" foreign policy, what this means is that since 1945 the dominant majorities in both major parties have agreed on the fundamentals of U.S. foreign policy. From 1945 to today, this policy has been continuous and reasonably coherent, and has never really wavered with a change in the presidency. That said, it should be noted that each of the two parties has a significant group within it which seeks to shift the emphasis of foreign policy in important ways. The Democratic Party has a (left) wing that tends to be more "dovish" (that is, influenced by the peace movement) and more sympathetic to the needs and claims of non-European zones of the world. This is what split the Democratic Party at the time of the Vietnam War.

The Republican Party has a counterpart in its (right) wing, which stresses two themes: on the one hand, a greater isolationism (rejection of the United Nations, unwillingness to spend money on aid projects, skepticism about sending troops anywhere to "keep the peace") and, on the other, macho militarism (more money for the armed forces, and particularly for weapons systems; aggressive impatience with development of military forces by anyone else, including so-called allies; tough stances toward China and Russia).

It is widely observed that Bush has a delicate political job holding together the diverse groups of his supporters, even on domestic issues. So far, he has indicated that he will handle the tensions by throwing bones to each camp, and by using slippery rhetoric. And so far (during the election) it has worked. The question is whether this tactic will work as well on foreign policy issues, especially given the fact that Bush does not command a clear majority in the U.S. Congress.

He has comforted the adepts of traditional U.S. policy by picking a foreign policy/defense/economy team drawn from his father's administration. And the appointment of Robert Zoellick as U.S. trade representative may be seen as public assurance that Bush will continue the "globalization" thrust of his predecessor. But he has not forgotten the other tendencies in the Republican Party. In Colin Powell, the U.S. now has a secretary of state who incarnates caution, even extreme caution, in the use of U.S. troops elsewhere in the world. And in Donald Rumsfeld, the U.S. now has a secretary of defense totally committed to creating the so-called National Missile Defense (NMD) system.

Powell and Rumsfeld are not extremists representing respectively the "isolationist" and "macho military" points of view, but neither do they represent a real brake on these tendencies. Furthermore, it should be underlined that there is a certain contradiction, at least on a tactical level, in pursuing these two tendencies simultaneously. Contradiction, and therefore confusion. And therefore nervousness elsewhere in the world.

In the short period since Bush was proclaimed the victor, the nervousness has expressed itself publicly in a number of ways. The South Koreans have indicated that they worry that Bush will not continue the initiatives toward North Korea undertaken by Clinton, thereby undermining the "sunshine" policy of Kim Dae-Jong. Lee Kuan Yew of Singapore, who is devoted to maintaining a U.S. role in Asia but also, behind the scenes, has been working to overcome the distance between the Chinese governments in Beijing and Taiwan, has indicated his fear that pursuing the NMD would in effect scuttle hopes that their differences could be bridged.

At the very moment the Bush team has been suggesting that it wants to get "tougher" with Saddam Hussein, Great Britain, the last ally of the United States in its policy in the region, has admitted that it is pressing the U.S. to end the "no overfly" policy in the southern and northern thirds of Iraq, which the U.S. and Great Britain are unilaterally enforcing.

Most of the world's immediate nervousness centers around the NMD. The prime minister of Canada has indicated diplomatically his complete lack of enthusiasm. And virtually no one in Europe thinks it is anything but a balmy idea. It is this which explains the Europeans' somewhat exaggerated response to the uncovering of the toxic damage wreaked by U.S. forces' use of "depleted uranium" in their weapons in Kosovo. I say "exaggerated" not because I don't think it was as irresponsible to use these such weapons as to use poison gas. I do. Rather, the response is exaggerated because many of the European governments have known about these dangers for a long time.

The real point here is that the U.S. seems to think that NATO constitutes a structure which constrains all its members to act together, except the United States. The Italian government is thus understandably upset that its soldiers have, as a consequence, contracted leukemia. And of course, not the Italians alone. The French seem to be playing the role of saying publicly what other Europeans are thinking privately. On January 10, the president of the Defense Commission of the French National Assembly, Paul Quilès, asserted that this affair illustrates "one of the essential problems of NATO," namely that "the Americans, within the framework of the Atlantic alliance, remain prone to take decisions unilaterally, without informing their partners, even after the event."

The U.S. is not fooled about what lies behind the debate on "depleted uranium" weapons. It is really the structure, indeed the very existence, of NATO. Donald Rumsfeld has already, in his testimony before Congress on his confirmation, stated his strong opposition to an autonomous European army, which, he said, would threaten the structure of NATO.

Where will all this lead? Clinton did his best to slow down the inevitable decline of U.S. power in the world. The Bush team thinks he didn't do enough. It is going to make adjustments. The result will probably be that it speeds up the process.

April 1, 2001: *"The Militarist Camp in the U.S."*

George W. Bush has made it quite clear, quite rapidly, that his administration will govern the United States as far to the right as it politically can. How far can it? To answer that, it is not enough to look at the balance of political forces between the Democrats and the Republicans. Most commentators seem to emphasize how closely the two parties are balanced at the moment in the U.S. Congress. This is the wrong way to look at it. The fact is that this is the first time in forty years and only the second time since 1932 that the Republican Party has controlled the presidency and *both* Houses of Congress. Numbers of bills that the Republicans favored in the last six years and for which they had the votes in Congress were either vetoed by Clinton or withdrawn in the face of a threatened veto. The Republicans are today in a relatively strong position, despite the closeness of the presidential election and despite the narrow margins they have in the legislature.

The real political question to look at is potential struggles within the Republican Party. Thus far, Bush has been able to hold the factions together, but can this last? Throughout the post-1945 period, there have always been three quite different constituencies comprising the Republican Party: the economic conservatives, the social conservatives, and the macho militarists. Of course, many individuals are all three, but most persons give priority to one of the three thrusts. And therein lies the problem for the Republicans.

The economic conservatives are mostly businessmen and their cadres plus high-earning professionals. Their priority at the moment is to reduce their tax burden and to resist any effort to force enterprises to internalize their costs (via ecological legislation). With amazing rapidity, Bush has indicated that he will fight very hard for everything this constituency wants. And it seems clearly to be his personal priority. He may not get everything he wants regarding tax reduction. But he will probably get almost everything he wants in terms of restricting environmental protection, since a large part of what is needed to be done requires the action of the executive branch of government. He has already repealed a good deal of what Clinton tried to put into effect in the closing days of his administration. And he has shut the door definitively on the Kyoto Protocol. To the Europeans (and Canadians), who are unanimously very upset, he has said unequivocally that the interests of U.S. businessmen are his first concern.

The social conservatives have played an increasingly important role in Republican politics over the last twenty-five years, due to the mobilization of the Christian Coalition. Bush has gone out of his way to make serious gestures toward meeting their demands. He has reinstated the ban on giving any money to any international organization that indicates in any way that it favors abortions. He has appointed one of them as the attorney-general, a key post. And he has in effect promised that his Supreme Court appointments would be ones they would favor. But he may not be able to get those appointments ratified. We shall see. However, in matters of new legislation, he has in effect told the social conservatives that they must do the work themselves to get the bills passed, and that, if they succeed, he promises to sign them. But it seems he is not going to spend too much of his own political ammunition in an effort to achieve these ends.

The joker in the pack is macho militarism. In a few short months, the Bush administration has managed to take on the entire world. Whereas the Clinton administration seemed to think that U.S. interests were served by calming down conflicts across the world (to be sure, in ways that the U.S. found comfortable), the Bush people almost appear to be stoking up the conflicts. They have said that a lot more has to be done about Saddam Hussein. They have withdrawn from mediating Israel/Palestine, and have shifted from a covertly pro-Israel position to an overtly pro-Israel, anti-Arafat position. They have flexed their muscles with the Canadians and the West Europeans by telling them in no uncertain terms that the U.S. will proceed with the new missile defense proposals, and have shown little interest in maintaining the old U.S.-Russian nuclear treaties, which they say are outdated. They have downgraded the Russians from being a potential ally to being again a potential enemy.

They seem to be on the point of giving Taiwan the kind of arms that they want and that the Chinese have made clear it is their priority for them not to get. As for easing anything on the Cuba embargo, forget it.

And of course, they seem determined to keep North Korea as an active enemy. This last posture has upset the European Union so much that it has sent a special delegation to North Korea, presumably to see if Europe could supply some of the financial assistance that the U.S. is clearly no longer ready to negotiate.

Romano Prodi, the president of the European Union Commission, has already accused the U.S. of failing to act like a "world leader" because of its narrow nationalist attitudes on the question of global warming. Mr. Bush seems oblivious. In his press conference of March 29, there occurred the following extraordinary exchange:

Question: Mr. President, allies of the United States have complained that you haven't consulted them sufficiently on your stance with negotiations with North Korea, Kyoto Treaty, your deteriorating relations elsewhere. If you strictly read the international press, it looks like everyone's mad at us. Mr. President, how do you think that came to be? And what, if anything, do you plan to do about it?

Answer: Well, I get a completely different picture, of course, when I sit down with the world leaders.

Bush then went on to say about the carbon dioxide issue that "we will not do anything that harms our economy, because first things first, are the people who live in America. That's my priority."

Is it really true that Bush is unaware of the fact that everyone is mad at the U.S., or does he not care? This is where the macho militarists come in. This group believes that power talks, and that if the U.S. doesn't act tough, it will lose everything—its power, its wealth, its centrality in the world-system. They don't want to settle conflicts; they want to win conflicts. And if it requires a little military action here or there, they are ready and eager.

The big question is, Are the American people eager or even ready? And even more important for Bush, are the businessmen, who are his basic support group and the group to which he owes his loyalty, ready? Because, although military armaments generate a lot of profits (Shaw explained all this wonderfully in *Major Barbara*), it is also true that unnecessary wars interfere with capitalist profits in many different ways (Schumpeter always argued this). One of the major reasons Clinton (and, before him, Bush the father) improved relations with China was the pressure of Republican businessmen, who wanted to invest and trade there. And it was Republican farm interests that pressed Clinton to ease the Cuban embargo. The militarist wing of the Republican Party runs against the grain of the economic conservative wing (or at least a part of it).

So the macho militarists may find arrayed against them not merely those they regard as their enemies (say, China and Russia) and the major U.S. allies but also perhaps some major transnationals and other large U.S. businesses. This may induce Bush to rein in the macho militarists, because if he doesn't they might escalate the provocations. Is Bush strong enough to do this?

Teddy Roosevelt, unabashed spokesman of U.S. imperialism, advised: "Speak softly and carry a big stick." The Bush people are not following this advice. They are speaking quite loudly indeed. But what is the size of their stick?

September 15, 2001: "*September 11, 2001—Why?*"

On September 11, 2001, the whole world watched as a dramatic human tragedy unfolded in the U.S., and everyone was fixated on it. Four commercial airliners were hijacked in the early morning. Four to five hijackers were aboard each plane. Armed with knives, and having at least one person among them capable of piloting the plane (at least, once it was in the air), the hijackers took over the planes, ousted (or killed) the pilots, and directed the planes on suicide missions. Three of the planes hit their targets: the two towers of the World Trade Center in New York City and the Pentagon in Washington.

Given both the amount of fuel aboard and the technical knowledge of the height at which the planes should hit the buildings, the hijackers managed to destroy the two towers completely and to carve a big hole in the Pentagon. As of now, there are probably more than 5,000 dead (no one has an exact figure) and many more hurt and traumatized. The U.S. air network and financial institutions have ground virtually to a halt, at least for this week, and untold short-range and middle-range economic damage has been done.

The first thing to note about this attack is its audacity and its remarkable success. A group of persons, linked together by ideology and willingness to be martyrs, engaged in a clandestine operation that must be the envy of any secret service agency in the world. They obtained entry into the United States and managed to carry knives onto four airplanes, which were leaving from three airports almost simultaneously, and all of which were heading out on transcontinental flights and therefore had large amounts of fuel on board. Three of the four planes reached their targets. Neither the CIA nor the FBI nor U.S. military intelligence nor anyone else had any advance notice or was able to do anything to stop this group.

The outcome was the most devastating event in the history of what we call terrorist attacks. No previous such attack killed more than 400 or so persons. Even at Pearl Harbor, to which the analogy is being widely made, and where the attack was conducted by the military forces of a state, many fewer people were killed. Furthermore, this was the first time since the Civil War (1861—1865) that warfare occurred within the boundaries of the continental United States. The U.S. has since been engaged in many major wars—the Spanish-American War, the First World War, the Second World War, Korea, and Vietnam (not to speak of "minor" wars)—and in all of them the actual fighting occurred outside these boundaries. What shocked the American people most of all about this attack was the fact that warfare occurred in the streets of New York and Washington.

So the big question is, Why? Virtually everyone is saying that the person responsible for the attack is Osama bin Laden. It seems a plausible assumption, since he has declared his intention to carry out such acts, and perhaps in the near future U.S. authorities will produce some evidence substantiating this assumption. Let us suppose it is correct. What would bin Laden hope to achieve in attacking the U.S. in this spectacular way? Well, 9/11 could be seen as an expression of anger and revenge for what bin Laden (among others) considers the misdeeds of the U.S. throughout the world, particularly in the Middle East. Would bin Laden think that, by committing such an act, he could persuade the U.S. government to change its policies? I seriously doubt that he is so naive as to believe this would be the reaction. President Bush says he regards the attack as an "act of war" and possibly bin Laden, if he is the perpetrator, thinks the same. Wars are conducted not to persuade the opponent to change his ways but to force him to do so.

So let us reason as though we were bin Laden. What has he proved by this attack? The most obvious thing he has proved is that the United States, the world's only superpower, the state with the most powerful and most sophisticated military hardware in the world, was unable to protect its citizens from this attack. Clearly, what bin Laden wished to do (again, presuming he is in fact the force behind 9/11) is to show that the U.S. is a paper tiger. And he wished to show it, first of all, to the American people, and then to everyone else in the world.

Now this is as obvious to the U.S. government as it is to bin Laden. Hence the response. President Bush says he will react forcefully, and the U.S. political elite of both parties have given him their patriotic assent without any hesitation. But now let us reason from the viewpoint of the U.S. government. What can it do?

The easiest thing is to obtain diplomatic support of condemnation of the attack and justification of any future counterattack. This is exactly what Secretary of State Powell said he would be doing. And the decision to do so is reaping its rewards. NATO has said that, under Article 5 of the treaty, a military attack on the U.S. (which NATO considers this to be) requires all its members to give military support to the counteraction, if the U.S. requests it. Every government in the world, including those of Afghanistan and North Korea, has condemned the attack. The sole exception is Iraq. It is true that popular opinion in Arab and Muslim states has not been as supportive of the U.S., but the U.S. will ignore that.

The fact that the U.S. has achieved this diplomatic support, which perhaps later will take the form of a U.N. resolution, hardly makes bin Laden quake in his boots. The diplomatic support will seem to be thin gruel for the American people as well. They will demand more. And "more" almost inevitably means some kind of military action. But what kind? Whom will the U.S. Air Force bomb? If bin Laden is behind 9/11, there are only two possible targets, depending on further knowledge about the evidence: Afghanistan and/or Iraq. How much damage will that do? In half-destroyed Afghanistan, military action hardly seems worthwhile. And the U.S. has been restrained about bombing Iraq for many reasons, including the wish not to lose lives. Maybe the U.S. will bomb someone. Will that convince the American people and the rest of the world that the U.S. is too fearsome to attack? Somehow I doubt it.

The truth of the matter is that there is not much the U.S. can do. The CIA tried for years to assassinate Castro, and he's still there. The U.S. has been searching for bin Laden for some years now, and he's still there. One day, U.S. agents may kill him, which might slow down this particular operation. It would also give great satisfaction to many people. But the problem would remain.

Obviously, the only thing to do is something political. But what? Here all accord within the U.S. (or, more widely, within the pan-Western arena) disappears. The hawks say this proves that Sharon and the present Israeli government are right: "They" are all terrorists, and the way to handle them is with harsh riposte. This hasn't been working so well for Sharon thus far. Why will it work better for George W. Bush? And can Bush get the American people to pay the price? Such a hawkish mode does not come cheaply. On the other hand, the doves are finding it difficult to make the case that the situation can be handled by "negotiation." Negotiation with whom, and with what end in view?

Perhaps what is happening is that this "war"—as it is being called this week in the press—cannot be won and will not be lost, but will simply continue. The disintegration of personal security is now a reality that may be hitting the American people for the first time. It was already a reality in many other parts of the world. The political issue underlying these chaotic oscillations of the world-system is not civilization versus barbarity (indeed, what we must realize is that all sides think they are the civilized ones, and that the barbarian is the other). Rather, it is the crisis in our world-system and the battle about what kind of successor world-system we would like to build.[1] This does not make it a contest between Americans and Afghans or Muslims or anyone else. It is a struggle between different visions of the world we want to build. September 11, 2001, contrary to what many are saying, will soon seem a minor episode in a long struggle that will continue to be a dark period for most people on this planet.

September 20, 2001: *"Beware! The United States Might Prevail"*

"If [bin Laden] thinks he can run and hide from the United States and our allies he will be sorely mistaken. ... We will prevail" (George W. Bush). There is an old peasant folk wisdom that says "beware of what you wish for; you may get it." I have little doubt that the United States is capable of bombing Afghanistan, overthrowing the Taliban, and killing bin Laden. The U.S. may prevail. And then what?

We prevailed once before in Afghanistan. In the 1980s, the country had a Communist government. The U.S. was

---

1. I have made the case for why we are living in a crisis of the world-system in *Utopistics, or Historical Choices for the Twenty-first Century* (New York: New Press, 1998).

unhappy and sought to overthrow it. The U.S. succeeded. The result? The U.S. got the Taliban and bin Laden,
whose organization is built on the foundation of CIA-
trained veterans of the anti-Communist struggle in Afghanistan.

At the time, there were Communist governments in
Bulgaria and Laos as well. The U.S. did not try to over-
turn them. Today, Bulgaria has a post-Communist government with the son of the former king as prime
minister. Not an impossible scenario for Afghanistan.
Today Laos, a very poor country, still with a Communist
government, is limping its way into involvement in the
world-economy. It is a threat to no one, not even the
U.S. Not an unlikely scenario for Afghanistan. But in
Afghanistan the U.S. insisted on prevailing.

How is the U.S. going to prevail now? Through a
combination of U.S. military might and support from
other countries. The U.S. has already announced that it
is insisting that all countries in the Middle East and the
Muslim world choose sides and support the U.S. uncon-
ditionally. Apparently, Pakistan has already agreed to
do this. The U.S. policy in the region has been based on
virtually unconditional support for Israel. But to an equal
extent it has been based on supporting the twin towers
of U.S. strength in the Islamic world—the regimes in
Saudi Arabia and Pakistan.

Saudi Arabia and Pakistan have different politics,
different locations, and different histories. But they share
two features. They are powerful and influential in the
whole region, and they have served U.S. interests extremely well over the past few decades. And the regimes in both countries are based on a coalition of
support from pro-Western modernizing elites and an
extremely conservative, popularly based Islamic establishment. These regimes have maintained their stability

because they have been able to juggle this combination. And they have been able to do so because of the ambivalence of their policies and their public pronouncements.

The United States is now saying "away with ambiguities." The U.S. may indeed prevail. But in the process, the regimes in Saudi Arabia and Pakistan may find that their popular base is irremediably eroded. They may collapse, just like the Twin Towers in New York City. And if they do, just like the Twin Towers, they will bring down other smaller buildings and weaken the foundations of still more. The United States may regret the day when Assad, Khaddafi, Arafat, and even Saddam Hussein are no longer in power. Their successors may be far fiercer in their anti-Americanism, inasmuch as they will no longer share modernist values with the United States. Consider that this may have been bin Laden's plan. His own suicide mission may have been to lead the United States into this trap.

October 1, 2001: "*The Outcome Could Not Be More Uncertain*"

In his speech to the U.S. Congress and to the world, President Bush said, in asserting what the U.S. intended to do, that there were many difficulties ahead, "yet its outcome is certain." This could not be more untrue. If his statement was meant as hortatory rhetoric, it may be considered normal discourse for a leader of a nation besieged. But if it reflects the analytic view of Bush and his principal deputies, then it is a dangerous misperception.

Of course, the first obscurity is to which outcome Bush is referring. He may mean the destruction of al-Qaeda, which is a possible albeit extremely difficult objective. He may mean the elimination or defanging of all groups anywhere that the U.S. will designate as "terrorist," in which case the possibility of success seems extremely dubious. He may mean a restoration of the belief of the American people and the world in general in the U.S. government's military prowess, which, at this point, is an objective whose success is quite uncertain. He may mean sustaining the interests of the United States as a country and of its enterprises, an objective whose likelihood of success is at best shaky.

It is important, when thinking about "outcomes," to give oneself different timelines. I propose three: six months, five years, fifty years. The picture for Bush looks rosiest within a six-months perspective. Consider what he has already gained in the short period since September 11. Before that day, the Bush administration was subjected to opposition, of varying degrees, from just about everywhere—notably, from the Democrats in Congress; the allies in Europe; Russia and China; the governments and populations of most of the countries in Asia, Africa, and Latin America; and the worldwide "anti-globalization" movement. That's a formidable list, and almost all of this opposition has either disappeared or been greatly muted since 9/11. The Democrats in Congress and the allies in Europe have rallied round the U.S. under siege. Russia, China, and most of the governments of Asia, Africa, and Latin America have given at least qualified support to a U.S. response to the attack. The "anti-globalization" movement has been relatively quiet and is wondering whether it should transform itself into a "peace" movement.

Of course, Bush is not the only one to derive some immediate political advantage from the attack. Since the U.S. is so anxious to line up everyone everywhere on its side, at least minimally, it has been ready to pay a diplomatic price in exchange, and others have not been hesitant to ask, especially those further away from the inner core of "friends." The Democrats in Congress and the allies in Western Europe have not yet dared to demand anything. But Russia, China, Pakistan, Sudan, the various Arab states (and whomever else Powell has been promising things) have been less bashful. And soon the Democrats and the allies in Western Europe may join in the game. So, for the moment, it sounds like a win-win game for everyone whom Osama bin Laden doesn't appreciate.

However, the bill comes due in six months. By then, the U.S. will have had to do something—something military. What it is we don't know for sure, and it seems that even the U.S. government may not know for sure. This is because, as has been widely admitted, there are no good options. A surgical strike against bin Laden by special troops parachuting into Afghanistan runs the risk of repeating the U.S. fiasco in Iran in 1980, which lost Carter his reelection. Bombing Afghanistan, the most probable single act, has multiple limitations: few plausible targets, a high likelihood of great civilian carnage plus a refugee flood into Pakistan, great political discomfort in Muslim states, and a low likelihood that bombing alone would end Taliban control of central Afghanistan.

There are some in the U.S. administration who want to bomb Iraq, which at least has plausible targets. The problem is that Saddam Hussein is not an ally of Osama bin Laden; more plausibly, he is one of the bin Laden's future targets. And bombing Iraq would not only undo all of Powell's efforts to create a grand coalition but also place the U.S. before the same dilemma it faced in 1991: Would it dare assume the burden of a land invasion and occupation?

And when the U.S. decides which of these doubtfully effective alternatives to choose, then what? If it "fails" militarily, this will reinforce bin Laden's point that the U.S. is a paper tiger, and we all know how fickle allies become when a great power demonstrates military weakness. If it doesn't fail in its actions *per se* but gets embroiled in a long military confrontation, any of the following may occur: significant loss of U.S. lives (bringing on all the internal U.S. debates about escalation that pervaded the Vietnam War); great civilian destruction in Afghanistan (which might make the world think that the 7,000 lives lost in the September 11 attack did not justify such a massive response); and great political turmoil in some Muslim countries—Pakistan, Saudi Arabia, Indonesia, Egypt, Algeria, Lebanon, Palestine, and others less obvious.

None of this would look good for the U.S. government. Suddenly, there might be a vast "peace" movement in the world. And George W. Bush might reflect, as Lyndon Johnson did, that it would be prudent not to run again.

Of course, this picture may be exaggerated. Perhaps the U.S. could in fact pull off a surgical strike. Perhaps the Taliban would collapse conveniently by themselves. Perhaps Bush would come out as a victorious hero, as his father did in 1991. At that point, he would still face two other hurdles.

One hurdle would be domestic. His father went from victory and incredible poll ratings to an electoral defeat within eighteen months because, as the saying went then, "It's the economy, stupid." Just this week, the *Wall Street Journal*, the incarnation of economic conservatism in the U.S., said that Secretary of the Treasury Paul O'Neill risked losing all his credibility because of his rosy optimism about the economy. Clearly, a lot of U.S. capitalists are hunkering down for the stormy period ahead. U.S. voters notoriously have a short memory and, once the flag-waving has passed, will vote their pocketbooks. And they always blame the ins for economic troubles.

If that weren't enough, suppose the U.S. took out bin Laden and overthrew the Taliban but then, three months later, somebody else was able to pull off a spectacular attack, in the U.S. or in Western Europe: Would not all the U.S. credit for success disappear in a puff of smoke? Certainly, the country's bravado and the self-confidence would be shaken. Is this so implausible?

Moving to a five-year perspective, we might then ask: Will the U.S. position in the world-system be stronger than it is today? Will the current geopolitical line-ups survive as a serious mode of organizing global politics? And will the "anti-globalization" movement perhaps metamorphose into something more coherent and far more militant than it is now? These are not unreasonable questions to consider. Others follow: Will chaotic conditions become the universal norm, and insecurity the daily potion of still more of us? Will the world-economy begin to oscillate wildly? And if it does, where will we be fifty years from now? Nothing could be less certain. But looking back from a half-century ahead, it is doubtful that even September 11 will seem all that important.

President Bush, in that same speech to Congress, said: "And we know that God is not neutral." I guess Bush is not known as a theologian. I thought that the way the three great Western religions—Judaism, Christianity, and Islam—had all dealt with the problem of evil ("If God is omnipotent, why does He permit evil to exist?) had been by saying that God had endowed humans with free will. But if God is not neutral, then humans do not have free will. And if humans have free will, then God is distinctly neutral about human conflicts.

October 15, 2001: "*The Dilemmas of a Superpower*"

President Bush and his associates have obviously been debating intensely how they should deal with the challenge to U.S. power and security that the September 11 attack has posed. They seem to be doing this carefully, and are probably quite dismayed at the negative consequences of most of the ways in which the U.S. government might react.

The first problem they have faced is the breadth of the "coalition" that the U.S. wishes to assemble in its "war on terrorism." The world press reports constantly that there are two quite different views within the U.S. government. Option A seems to be broad coalition and narrow definition of objectives. Option B seems to be narrow coalition and broad definition of objectives. The press indicates that Colin Powell is the most prominent spokesperson for Option A and that Undersecretary of Defense Paul Wolfowitz is the most prominent spokesperson for Option B. For the moment, it seems that President Bush, Vice-President Cheney, and probably Secretary of Defense Rumsfeld have come down on the side of Option A, and that is what the U.S. is initially pursuing.

What does Option A involve? It involves trying to get virtually every government in the world to endorse the objective of pursuing bin Laden. That is of course not difficult, since bin Laden and al-Qaeda seem to have negative views about virtually every government in the world, with the exception of the Taliban. They denounce the U.S. above all, and Israel too, of course. But they also denounce Russia, China, Saudi Arabia, Pakistan, Egypt, and Iran. They do not like the Iraqi regime. Small wonder that virtually all of these governments return the compliment. The objective, "bringing bin Laden to justice," gets rapid endorsement.

But how does one bring bin Laden to justice? It seems that the answer is to put pressure on the Taliban, who are the de facto (if not the de jure) government of Afghanistan. What kind of pressure? Well, bombing. A little bombing has won at least tacit support from the "coalition." A lot of bombing? We shall have to see. And extending the bombing to include Iraq, as proponents of Option B wish to do? Very few governments would endorse that.

The United States has not ruled out Option B. It seems merely to have decided to try Option A first. President Bush has been careful to add sentences to his statements that leave the door slightly open to Option B. They have also left the door open in a second way: The coalition may be as wide as conceivable, but the military action includes only two countries, the U.S. and Great Britain.

This is no accident. At the time of the Gulf War, the first President Bush asked for U.N. authorization. The U.S. found that this meant it had to clear various matters along the route with too many others. So, when Kosovo came along, President Clinton was careful to leave the United Nations out and to ask only for NATO authorization. It turned out that, as far as the U.S. government was concerned, even NATO tied U.S. military hands too much. This time, when NATO offered its military help, the U.S. said no. Germany is reported to have been particularly peeved. Doing it this way, however, means that if the U.S. decides to move to Option B, it has to get clearance from Tony Blair. (The press suggests, however, that even Blair might not be enthusiastic about extending action to Iraq.)

What is this all about? Since bin Laden has openly challenged the U.S.'s military prowess, the U.S. is determined to reassert exactly that. It's not merely a matter of protecting U.S. citizens and residents from attack, but also of reestablishing worldwide belief that the U.S. is an invincible superpower. Can the U.S. do this?

The problem with Option A is that bombing raids on Afghanistan are not going to accomplish much. Probably the next step will be sending in special forces. Bin Laden knows that and, indeed, looks forward to it. He seems convinced that the Afghans defeated the Soviet Union and brought down its system. Of course, the U.S. believes *it* brought down the Soviet Union, but that is not bin Laden's view. Bin Laden clearly hopes, and expects, that the U.S. will meet the Soviet fate in Afghanistan, and that as a consequence he will "bring down" the United States as a superpower. It seems a fantastic idea, but then bringing down the Twin Towers in New York would have been considered a fantastic idea a mere two months ago.

Bush, Rumsfeld, and Blair have been repeating, almost as a litany, that the war will be "long," and by that they seem to mean at the very least a year (or two or three?). They are thus "preparing" U.S. and world public opinion for the fact that instant victory is not at hand. The problem with a "long" war is that the very length of it works in favor of bin Laden's objective: exposing the clay feet of a superpower. If the war is long (and begins to be costly in terms of lives lost), without clear military achievements, a number of things will happen. The "coalition"—particularly the degree of support the U.S. will be able to get from Pakistan and Saudi Arabia—will fritter away. A "peace movement" will begin to emerge in the U.S., the Western world more generally, and the rest of the world as well.

But perhaps worst of all for the Bush administration, it might begin to be torn apart itself. The proponents of Option B will become more vocal and more denunciatory of the proponents of Option A. Who knows who would then resign? But such a development cannot be politically healthy for President Bush. If, in addition, there were one or two coups in Middle Eastern states that brought to power governments less friendly to the U.S., the situation would only be exacerbated. And if violence escalated on other fronts (not only Israel/Palestine but, say, northern Ireland, Indonesia, and who knows where else?), the idea that bin Laden was the singular most evil "terrorist" in the world would begin to seem implausible.

This is of course a dismal picture from the viewpoint of the U.S. government. The proponents of Option B will say that such an outcome is by no means inevitable. They will urge not only Option B but perhaps an enhanced version—say, using tactical nuclear weapons somewhere or other. This is not an impossible scenario. If carried out, however, it could isolate the U.S. diplomatically in a dramatic way. On the other hand, the U.S. could find itself less capable of maintaining diplomatic support even if it stayed with Option A but were not able to eliminate bin Laden.

The United States is playing for very high stakes. It had lured itself into thinking, after the collapse of the Soviet Union, that it was truly a superpower, and that no force could stand in its way. It misinterpreted its very limited victories in the Gulf War and in Kosovo as evidence that this was true. It may well find out that it isn't. And if that happens, then it may have to reassess quite dramatically how it relates to the rest of the world. Bin Laden claims to speak for long-standing grievances of the Islamic world. He envisages a replacement world in which very few of us could find a place, or would find livable. It would not be a better world, even for Muslims. But bin Laden is a clever man as well as an ideologically committed man, who is taking great advantage of the structural weaknesses of the U.S. position as a declining hegemonic power. And it is not at all clear that the U.S. governments (of either Bush or Clinton before him) have understood geopolitical realities as well as he and al-Qaeda have. In war and diplomacy, there is no room for self-deception.

November 1, 2001: *"Superpower?"*

The United States is a hegemonic power in decline. I have been expressing this viewpoint since at least 1980.[2] The statement is meant to be analytic and not prescriptive. I have found that nonetheless it evokes not only disbelief but anger, and that such a reaction occurs on all sides of the political spectrum, and all around the world. Persons on the right take the statement to be false, or rather they take it to be true only insofar as the superpower has insufficiently asserted its strength. Furthermore, they seem to assume that, by making such an analysis, I am creating a defeatist attitude that is self-fulfilling. These persons have a strange belief in the power of the word, or at least of my word.

Persons on the left are often incredulous, telling me it is obvious that the United States dominates the world scene and imposes itself around the world, in evil ways. So how can I talk of the U.S. being in decline? Am I not thereby deflecting people from meaningful action? And persons in the center seem to be offended by the very idea that appropriate intelligent action on the part of those in power will not, cannot, eventually remedy any limitations on U.S. virtuous action.

---

2. I believe the first time I said this was in "Friends as Foes," *Foreign Policy*, No. 40 (Fall 1980), pp. 119–131.

What does it mean to be a hegemonic power? Such a power normally defines the rules of the geopolitical game and gets its way almost all of the time simply by political pressure, without having to resort to the actual use of force. The story of how one gets to be a hegemonic power and why it is that hegemony never lasts is not my subject here.[3] The question, rather, is what evidence do I have that U.S. hegemony is on the wane.

I certainly do not deny that the U.S. today is the strongest military power in the world, and that by far. This is true not just today but probably for at least another twenty-five years. However, it is no longer true that the U.S. unilaterally defines the rules of the geopolitical game, nor it is true that it gets its way most of the time simply by political pressure, or even gets its way most of the time. The present struggle with bin Laden is not the first, but merely the latest, instance of this new reality.

I say "new reality" because there was a time not so long ago when the U.S. was truly hegemonic, when it was the only superpower. This was more or less the case between 1945 and 1970. Despite the cold war and despite the U.S.S.R. (or maybe in large part because of them), the U.S. almost always could get what it wanted, where it wanted, when it wanted. It ran the United Nations. It kept the Soviet Union contained within the borders the Red Army had reached in 1945. It used the CIA to oust or rearrange governments it found unfriendly (Iran in 1953, Guatemala in 1954, Lebanon in 1956, the Dominican Republic in 1965, and so on). It imposed its will on often reluctant allies in Western Europe, forcing them to pull back from military operations (as in Suez

---

3. I first treated this question in "The Three Instances of Hegemony in the History of the Capitalist World-Economy," reprinted in *The Politics of the World-Economy* (Cambridge: Cambridge University Press, 1984), pp. 37–46.

in 1956) or pressing them to speed up the pace of decolonization because the U.S. considered this to be the wiser and safer course.

In this period, Americans were learning how to "assume their responsibilities" in the world. They had a "bipartisan" foreign policy. Then things began to change. The big economic lead the U.S. had over Western Europe and Japan disappeared. These countries became economic rivals, while remaining political allies. The U.S. began to lose wars. It lost the war in Vietnam in 1973. It was humiliated by Khomeini in Iran in 1980. President Reagan withdrew U.S. marines from Lebanon in 1982 because over 200 of them were killed in a terrorist attack (and this two days after he had said that the U.S. would never do this). The Gulf War was a draw, the troops returning back to the line where it began. Some Americans say today that this was because the U.S. didn't have the guts to march on Baghdad (or made the mistake of not doing so). But the decision of the first President Bush reflected a military-political judgment that the march would have led to a U.S. disaster over time, a judgment that seems solid and prudent. And whereas Jimmy Carter could impose a Camp David settlement on Egypt and Israel in 1978, Bill Clinton could not do the same for Palestine and Israel in 2000, although he tried hard enough.

The last time the U.S. snapped its fingers and got its way was on September 11, 1973, when it engineered a coup in Chile and put Pinochet in power. On September 11, 2001, it was bin Laden who snapped his fingers, and the U.S. people and government are still reeling from the blow. Now, bin Laden does not have a large army or navy or air force. His technological capacity is relatively primitive. He does not have funds available to him that can match U.S. government resources. So, even if the match were to end in a draw, he will have won.

It took the U.S. thirty years to learn how to "assume its responsibilities" as a hegemonic power. It wasted the next thirty years, pining for lost glory and maneuvering to hold on to as much of the power as it could. Perhaps it should spend the next thirty years learning how to be a rich, powerful country in an unequal world, but one in which it no longer controls the situation unilaterally. In such a world, it would have to learn how to come to terms with the rest of the world (not only Afghanistan, not even only China and Russia, but also Canada, Western Europe, and Japan).

In the collapsing world anarchy that is marking the transition from our modern world-system to something else, how the United States—its government, its citizens, its large enterprises—plays its roles matters to everyone. Everyone everywhere has an interest in obtaining an intelligent, creative, hopeful response from the United States to the world crisis in which we all find ourselves today. For the U.S. is still the strongest power in the world, and it still has traditions and aspirations that it values and that many people (not only Americans) think have contributed something positive to the world in which we all live.

The ball is in the United States' court. It is too easy for Americans to be infuriated at the terrible destruction of human lives in the Twin Towers tragedy and its aftermath. There is too much unthinking anger in the world already (even if much of the anger on all sides is justified). There is no guarantee that the world can navigate the next twenty-five to fifty years with minimal violence. But we can try to analyze what it would take to get us all out of the deep hole in which we find ourselves these days.

December 15, 2001: "*The Swooping of the Hawks?*"

"Whom the Gods would destroy they first make mad" (Euripides).

The day of the hawks may be here. Poor hawks. They have been so frustrated by American presidents— and not merely by such Democratic wimps as Clinton and Carter. George W. Bush wouldn't send troops into China earlier this year when the Chinese had the audacity to down a U.S. plane that overflew their territory. George Bush, father, wouldn't march on Baghdad. Ronald Reagan himself virtually gave the crown jewels away at Reykjavik when he met with Gorbachev. Let's not even talk about Ford. And Richard Nixon (along with his sidekick Henry Kissinger) actually made a deal with Mao Zedong, not to speak of signing that dangerous 1972 ABM treaty. The last gutsy thing an American president did was to drop atomic bombs on Japan. And that was done by Harry ("give 'em hell") Truman.

But Osama bin Laden did the hawks the favor of mobilizing American nationalism behind their program of "America can do anything it wants in the world because America is the land of liberty, the only real land of liberty." And it looks like the hawks are going to go for broke. The U.S. government is withdrawing from the 1972 nuclear treaty. It is seriously considering war on Iraq, according to the clear warning of Vice-President Cheney. It has ended any semblance of impartiality in the Israel/Palestine imbroglio. And it is certainly twisting arms all around the world, trying to make sure no serious dissidence arises from its decisions.

For the moment, the U.S. public seems ready to back almost any macho assertion of U.S. power, anywhere.

What has succeeded is success. The U.S. armed might has undone the Kalashnikovs of a bunch of mad mullahs in Afghanistan and installed in power what is probably a bunch of mad warlords, but at least they're the U.S.'s warlords—for the moment, that is. And hey, fellas, all that matters is whether you're ready to cooperate with the Pentagon, isn't that so? Well, they seem for the moment to have ousted the mad mullahs. Come back in six months to be sure.

More than that, the U.S. public is ready to denounce as traitors (or almost) any U.S. citizens who are raising any questions about these policies. As the ostensible opposition, the Democrats in Congress are scared out of their wits that they might be targeted as less than enthusiastic about a militarist program that even Nixon and Reagan, not to speak of Bush the elder, wouldn't have touched when they were president. Ah, for the good old days, when all the U.S. had in power were Johnson and McNamara. The hawks are really serious these days—no moral twinges, no intellectual hesitations. If, while they're at it, they can seriously limit civil liberties within the U.S. and throw tens of billions of taxpayer dollars to the poor suffering megacorporations—well, all the better. But this is all secondary to showing the rest of the world that what the U.S. says goes, and those in the rest of the world better believe that it doesn't matter if they don't like it.

So, for the few sober types who are still around, let us try to calculate what will actually happen. Will the U.S. do it? Quite possibly. Why? Bombastic aggressiveness is usually a sign not of strength but of weakness. If the U.S. government really felt that everything was going its way, it wouldn't need to bomb Baghdad. One doesn't need to read Machiavelli or Gramsci to know that force is not the optimal way to control the world;

it's second best or third best. I will not review these arguments here, but simply assert again that the U.S. is today a hegemonic power in decline.

When a hegemonic power is in decline, it has only two plausible alternatives: Either adjust to reality intelligently, reaping the continuing rewards of past accumulation, or pull the house down. What our hawks are proposing is pulling the house down. Some of them may believe that they and their friends will survive Armageddon, and still be on top—with a little "collateral damage," to be sure. Others, more lucid, may not care (Après moi, le déluge!). And some may be Dr. Strangelove—mad!

We are living in a dangerous time. The hawks don't have it easy; they don't get that many opportunities. This is one of those rare moments. If they don't grab it, they may not get another chance like this for a long while. The implication, of course, is that if they are stopped now, the worst may pass. What does this depend upon?

It depends on the degree of awareness of the danger, not merely among the immediate targets of destruction but among all those who are supposedly in the camp of the U.S. government—the political center in the United States, the member-governments of NATO, the military leaders who understand the consequences. And it depends on the degree of intelligent and rapid mobilization of those Franklin Roosevelt called "left of center."

They all have been relatively mute these past three months—owing, in part, to the emotional events of September 11, the world's lack of sympathy with the methods and goals of Osama bin Laden, and, more recently, the seemingly rapid fadeaway of the Taliban. This is what the hawks have been counting on. The day of the hawks may be here, but if so, this is the moment to counter them with vigorous action.

April 1, 2002: *"Iraq: How Great Powers Bring Themselves Down"*

George W. Bush is a geopolitical incompetent. He has allowed a clique of hawks to induce him to take a position, on the invasion of Iraq, from which he cannot extract himself and which will have nothing but negative consequences for everyone concerned—but, above all, for the United States. He will find himself badly hurt politically, perhaps even destroyed. He will diminish rather rapidly the already declining power of the United States in the world. And he will contribute dramatically to the destruction of the state of Israel by furthering the suicidal madness of the Israeli hawks. Of course, there are many people in the world who will be happy to see such negative consequences. The trouble is that, in the process, Bush will conduct warfare that will destroy many lives immediately, lead to turmoil in the Arab-Islamic world of a kind and at a level hitherto unimagined, and perhaps unleash nuclear weapons that, once used, will be hard to make illegitimate after that. How have we all gotten into such a disastrous cul-de-sac?

It seems reasonable to assume that a U.S. military action against Iraq is now not a question of maybe but how soon. Why is this happening? If one asks spokespersons for the U.S. government, the reason given is that Iraq has been defying U.N. resolutions and represents an imminent danger to the world in general, and perhaps the U.S. in particular.

This explanation of the expected military action is so thin that it cannot be taken seriously. Acts of defiance against U.N. resolutions or other international enjoinders have been a dime a dozen for the last fifty years. I need hardly remind anyone that the U.S. refused to defer to a World Court decision about Nicaragua that condemned it. And President Bush has made it amply clear that he will not honor any treaty that he believes is dangerous to U.S. national interests. Israel has, of course, been defying U.N. resolutions for over thirty years, and is doing so again as I write this commentary. And the record of other U.N. members is not much better. So, yes, Saddam Hussein has been defying quite explicit U.N. resolutions. What else is new?

Is Saddam Hussein an imminent threat to anyone? In August 1990, Iraq invaded Kuwait. That action at least posed an imminent threat. The response was the so-called Persian Gulf War. In that war, the U.S. pushed the Iraqis out of Kuwait, and then decided to stop there. Saddam Hussein remained in power in Iraq. The U.N. passed various resolutions requiring Iraq to abandon nuclear, chemical, and bacteriological weapons, and mandated inspection teams to verify this. The U.N. also embargoed Iraq in various ways. As we know, over the decade since then, the de facto situation has changed, and the system of constraints on Iraq put in place by these U.N. resolutions has weakened considerably, though by no means totally.

On March 28, 2002, Iraq and Kuwait signed an agreement in which Iraq agreed to respect the sovereignty of Kuwait. The foreign minister of Kuwait, Sabah al-Ahmad al-Sabah, said his country is now "100% satisfied." Asked by a reporter if Kuwait was happy with each and every clause in the agreement, the foreign minister replied, "I wrote them myself." The spokesperson for the United States, however, exhibited skepticism. The U.S. is not about to be deterred simply because Kuwait is "satisfied." What is Kuwait, that it should participate in such a decision?

The U.S. hawks believe, as I have suggested repeatedly, that only the use of force, very significant force, will restore the U.S.'s unquestioned hegemony in the world-system. Undoubtedly, the use of overwhelming force does establish hegemony. This occurred in 1945, and the U.S. did become the hegemonic power. But the use of such force when the conditions of hegemony have already been undermined is a sign of weakness rather than of strength, and weakens the user. It is clear that, at this point, no one supports the U.S. invasion of Iraq: not a single Arab state, not Turkey or Iran or Pakistan, not a single European power.

There is, to be sure, one notable exception: Great Britain, or rather Tony Blair. Mr. Blair, however, is having two problems at home. There is a brewing revolt in the Labour Party. And, even more important, as *The Observer* of March 17 reported: "Britain's military leaders issued a stark warning to Tony Blair last night that any war against Iraq is doomed to fail and would lead to the loss of lives for little political gain." I cannot believe that U.S. military leaders are really making a different assessment, although they may be perhaps more wary of telling it "like it is" to President Bush. Kenneth Pollack, the Iraqi person in Clinton's Security Council, says that such a war would require sending in an initial 200,000–300,000 U.S. troops, presumably from bases in either Saudi Arabia or Kuwait, and then even more to defend the Kurds in northern Iraq. These troops would presumably come from, or fly over, Turkey.

The U.S. seems to be counting on intimidating all its "allies" into going along. After the occupation of Ramallah by Sharon, the remote hope that Saudi (or even Kuwaiti) bases would be available has probably disappeared. Turkey clearly does not want to defend Iraqi Kurds, when the major consequence of doing so would be to strengthen the Kurdish movement in Turkey, against which the Turkish government focuses all its efforts. As for Israel, Sharon seems to be intent on carrying out as rapidly as possible the reoccupation of the West Bank and Gaza and the destruction of the Palestinian Authority. And Bush gives him 99 percent support in this.

If my analysis is accurate, then there will be an invasion that will be difficult if not impossible to win, resulting in the loss of many lives (most notably U.S. lives) and culminating in a quasi-withdrawal by the U.S. A second Vietnam. Can no one in the Bush administration see this? A few, but they are not being counted. Why? Because Bush is in a self-imposed dilemma. If he goes ahead with the Iraq invasion, he will bring himself down, like Lyndon Johnson, or be humiliated, like Richard Nixon. And the U.S. failure will finally give the Europeans the courage to be European and not Atlantic. So why do it? Because Bush promised the U.S. people a "war on terrorism" that "we will certainly win."

So far, all he's produced is the downfall of the Taliban. He hasn't captured bin Laden. Pakistan is shaky. Saudi Arabia is pulling away. If he doesn't invade Iraq, he will look foolish where it matters to him most—in the eyes of American voters. And he is being told this, in no uncertain terms, by his advisors on internal U.S. politics. Bush's incredibly high ratings are those for a "war president." The minute he becomes a peacetime president, he will be in grave trouble, all the more so because of his failed wartime promises.

So, he has no choice. He will invade Iraq. And we shall all live with the consequences.

July 1, 2002: *"Preemption: The Political and Moral Stakes"*

War remains a reality of the world. Nonetheless, for five centuries at least, states within the modern world-system have been struggling to create "rules of war" that would somehow limit, even eliminate, the most brutal, least justified modes of engaging in warfare. These rules have been increasingly codified in international treaties.

In 1945, the United Nations Charter made a distinction between starting wars and defending one's country against wars that others started. The Charter accepts the legitimacy of "self-defense" and even of "collective self-defense"—that is, agreements between countries that if one is attacked, the others would rise to its defense. While in practice these rules have often been violated, it is the tribute of vice to virtue that violators since 1945 have hypocritically denied that they were violators. They have insisted that they did not start wars but that the other side did. For example, North Korea has always denied that it started a war with South Korea in 1950, arguing that it was South Korea that initiated hostilities. And when the United States invaded Grenada in 1983, it asserted that it was doing this only because the lives of U.S. medical students were endangered, and that therefore Grenada was the first to be hostile.

During the long cold war between the United States and the Soviet Union, there was said to be a "balance of terror"; in other words, both sides knew that, if the other started a war by using nuclear weapons, their side was in a position to respond effectively, and that therefore the principal result would be mutual destruction. Nonetheless, there was constant discussion within the U.S. government (and perhaps within the Soviet government as well) of whether or not it was possible and desirable to launch such a war with so much surprise that the other side would be unable to respond effectively. This plan of action was referred to as a "first strike" that would be "preemptive." It obviously never occurred. We cannot be sure whether the decisions were made primarily on technical grounds (the surprise would never be sufficient to avoid devastating response) or on political/moral grounds (a first strike would violate the U.N. Charter). What can be said is that no U.S. administration ever definitively repudiated the possibility of a first strike. Many persons believed that this was because each side wanted to keep the other on its toes and not because either side ever intended to carry one out.

After the collapse of the Soviet Union, it was argued that there was less need to worry about a "first strike" since the cold war was over. But since September 11, the subject has been revived. In his West Point speech in June 2002, President George W. Bush said: "If we wait for threats to fully materialize, we will have waited too long." This is fairly clear language. It says a first strike is legitimate, especially since Condoleeza Rice elaborated on the speech by saying: "It means forestalling certain destructive acts against you by an adversary."

Bob Woodward revealed, in the *Washington Post* of June 16, 2002, that the Bush administration has recently discussed the possible use of U.S. teams to assassinate Saddam Hussein. The U.S. had engaged in assassination attempts in the 1950s and 1960s—none successfully, as far as we know. As a result of the revelation of this policy by the Church Committee of the U.S. Senate in 1973, President Ford issued an executive order in 1976 banning the practice. This order was maintained by subsequent U.S. presidents, including Reagan and Bush (father). It is this order that is now being repealed.

In the latest issue of the *International Journal of Intelligence and Counterintelligence* (Vol. 15, No. 2, 2002), Jeffrey T. Richelson makes an open case for "assassination as a national security option." It is worth reviewing his arguments:

No convincing case can be made that the ban [on assassinations] should be made absolute. ... Arguing that the U.S.

should continue its ban in its present form would be more reasonable. Under the standing U.S. interpretation of international law, targeted killings of enemy leaders are permitted in just those situations where they are most likely to be indicated—in the midst of war, during a continuing series of terrorist attacks, or in the face of imminent attack. Thus, the ban did not stop President George W. Bush from signing a presidential finding in October 2001 that authorized the killing of Osama bin Laden.

So the plan seems clear. First, the U.S. attempts to assassinate Saddam Hussein. If that doesn't work (and it seems a bit unlikely that it will), then a preemptive first strike will be tried. President Bush has been quite ready to indicate that he desires "regime change" in various countries. To say that this is a violation of sovereignty is to say the obvious. But that doesn't seem to faze him, since he is speaking the language of power, not of law. Moreover, he is coating this language of power in the language of morality: the struggle against terrorism and for democracy. I shall not discuss here the political efficacy of such a policy. I have done that elsewhere, and, in any case, its political efficacy is precisely the subject of debate within the U.S. administration, the U.S. Congress, and the various leaders of the European Union.

But this is a question not only of politics but of law and of morality, and the two latter issues seem to be getting less debate. It seems clear to simple people (I am a simple person) that "forestalling" is not "defense" for one simple reason: The only way the law recognizes defense is *after* an act occurs. Intent to engage in an act does not constitute an act, since one never knows if the intent will be carried through. In addition, the forestaller is interpreting this intent, and he can (and quite often does) interpret it incorrectly. In criminal law, I am not legally authorized to shoot someone because I have heard him say nasty things about me and think that one day soon he may try to shoot me. If however, this other person points a gun at me, I may shoot him in self-defense. Without this elementary distinction, we are in a lawless world.

Then there is morality. Morality is dependent on the reasonableness of our actions. And reasonableness requires taking into account the degree to which we ourselves might be mistaken. There seems to be little indication that anyone in the U.S. administration is worrying about the fact that we might possibly be mistaken. But such worry, such self-analysis, is crucial to morality. A preemptive war is an irrevocable action. It is not a minor misdemeanor that can be rectified by, say, financial compensation. People die, and in most cases many people die. The preemptor may say he wishes to prevent others (his friends and family, his co-nationals) from dying in the expected aggression of the other. The fact remains, nonetheless, that the preemptor shoots first and kills first. If this is not covered by the commandment "Thou shalt not kill," what is?

So it seems to me absurdly simple. First strikes are against international law. First strikes are immoral. If they constitute a political error, we may survive that. An error in law (of this magnitude) undermines the very possibility of law. And an error in morality (some call it a sin) is one that transforms us, not visibly for the better.

July 15, 2002: "*Judge, Jury, and Cavalry*"

I have used as my title the headline of a story concerning the U.S. government's passionate opposition to the International Criminal Court (ICC), an article that appeared in Australia's leading newspaper, the *Sydney*

Morning Herald, on July 5, 2002. The world has seen recently the following extraordinary set of events. The ICC was established by an international treaty that was signed by the U.S. during the Clinton presidency. Clinton did not submit the treaty for ratification, partly because the U.S. armed forces were very unhappy with it and partly because it had no chance of being ratified by the U.S. Senate. He signed it nonetheless in order to give the U.S. the power to propose future amendments to the treaty.

When Bush came to power, the U.S. went further. Bush "unsigned" the treaty. This may not be legal, but it was done anyway, and in practice the unsigning was merely a rhetorical act. The treaty was due to come into operation only when sixty nations had ratified it. The U.S. had thought that this would not happen in less than ten years, but in fact it was achieved in two years, and the ICC came into formal existence on July 1, 2002. The treaty, as written, applies to all countries whether or not they are signatories. It provides, under specified circumstances and with many safeguards, for the possibility of pursuing people for acts violating the rules of war in a tribunal that will be located in The Hague in the Netherlands.

The U.S. government, as we say in good U.S. slang, went ballistic. It pulled out all the stops. The first concrete issue was the United Nations mandate to keep troops in Bosnia, which was due to be renewed on July 1. The U.S. vetoed this renewal because the U.N. Security Council refused to vote an explicit exemption from the provisions of the treaty for U.S. military and government personnel.

The U.S. has also threatened to veto all other U.N. peacekeeping missions that will come up for renewal or for creation. This includes, for example, the forces on the Israel-Lebanon border, which are what keeps Hezbollah somewhat away from the Israeli border and, up to now, has been a desideratum of the Sharon government. In addition, a committee of the U.S. Congress has already voted in a provision that would bar military aid to any country that ratified the treaty.

With whom is the U.S. quarreling? The so-called axis-of-evil countries are not signatories. China is not a signatory. The principal signatories and leading advocates of the ICC are all of the U.S.'s NATO allies. It was Great Britain and France that led the struggle against U.S. efforts in the Security Council to obtain a special exemption for the U.S. to the provisions of the treaty. There is talk that, should an American be brought before the ICC in The Hague, a rescue mission would be sent by the U.S. So we are envisaging U.S. marines landing in the Netherlands with hostile intent to "rescue" a U.S. citizen accused of war crimes.

This seems to be an Alice in Wonderland world. How to explain what has all the appearance of U.S. hysteria? It makes eminent sense, however, if one shares the logic of the U.S. hawks. The fact is that the creation of the ICC is indeed a further step in the creation of international law, and any such step is indeed an encroachment on existing sovereignty. It is meant to be that. Of course, as the West Europeans say, the treaty is designed to deal with egregious violations of existing international norms, the kind of crimes with which Milosevich is now charged before a special tribunal. Essentially, the ICC is a permanent tribunal of the same design. It is also true that the present treaty does provide that if an individual is charged with such a crime, jurisdiction lies first with that individual's national courts, and a case can be brought before the ICC only if the national courts do not consider the case. It is therefore highly unlikely that any

U.S. citizen would be brought before the ICC at the present time.

But the U.S. says two things. Times may change. And there are plenty of people in the rest of the world who bear a sufficient grudge against the U.S. so as to bring multiple accusations, one or more of which might eventually result in a case before the U.S. This is of course true. The issue is whether the U.S. wishes to rely upon the "law" to resolve such matters or whether it insists on being "judge, jury, and cavalry" in a lawless world.

The attitude of the present U.S. government has a long history behind it. The U.S. has always had a significant portion of the population and its political leadership who view international law and institutions with a jaundiced—indeed hostile—eye. This wing of opinion combines essential isolationism with essential militarism. Before 1941, this point of view had great strength within the Republican Party. (Those Democrats who were "isolationist" tended to be relatively pacifist.) There was of course an "internationalist" wing of the Republicans, associated with Wall Street, big business, and the East Coast, but they were always a minority.

The Second World War made isolationism unpopular and politically untenable. The famous conversion of Senator Arthur Vandenberg to the new structure of the United Nations constituted the political basis on which the so-called bipartisan foreign policy of the U.S. was built in the post-1945 years. Of course, the fact that there was a cold war to justify the "internationalism" helped considerably. The end of the cold war marked the end of a commitment by members of the U.S. right to "internationalism." They have returned publicly to their pre-1941 stance, a combination of isolationism and militarism. In this light, unless NATO is entirely compliant toward U.S. wishes, NATO is as much the enemy as the "axis of evil." This is what we are seeing in connection with discussion of the hypothetical sending of U.S. marines to invade the Netherlands.

Of course, this U.S. stance wreaks havoc with the efforts of the European Union (and Canada) to construct a "world order," in which the ICC plays an important role as an institution to further "human rights." The U.S. hawks have no interest whatsoever in such a world order. They are interested in asserting U.S. unilateral military power, and in imposing this power on everyone, not least on the NATO allies. The idea that a U.S. soldier could be called to account somewhere because he had committed an act violating international law and the norms of natural law is absolutely anathema to U.S. hawks. For, they say, after the trial of Sergeant X will come an accusation against Henry Kissinger or (why not?) George W. Bush.

A last-minute compromise has postponed the issue for one year. But this changes little. One of two things will happen now. Great Britain, France, and the others will bend, the ICC will be dismantled, and the U.S. will prevail as "judge, jury, and cavalry." Or they will not bend, and it may be NATO that is dismantled. This is not a minor quarrel.

September 1, 2002: *"George W. Bush, Principal Agent of Osama bin Laden"*

Osama bin Laden made it clear on September 11, 2001, that he wished to harm the United States grievously, and to bring down "bad Muslim" governments, most particularly those of Saudi Arabia and Pakistan. George W. Bush is working overtime to help him achieve both goals. Indeed, one might say that, without George W.

Bush, Osama bin Laden would not be able to achieve these objectives, at least in any short time horizon.

George W. Bush is preparing to invade Iraq. The opposition to this move is becoming impressive. First, within the United States, two groups have become very vocal in the last few weeks. One is what are referred to as the "old Bushies"—that is, George W. Bush's father and those who were his closest advisors. We have had very strong warnings from James A. Baker, Brent Scowcroft, and Lawrence Eagleburger—all part of the inner circle of the first President Bush's administration—that an invasion now, without U.N. authorization, is unwise, and furthermore unnecessary, and can have only negative consequences for the United States.

Then there is the opposition of the military. Brent Scowcroft is of course a former general. In addition, we have heard from Norman Schwarzkopf, who led the U.S. troops in the Gulf War; Anthony Zinni, who commanded all U.S. troops in the Middle East and has been the current administration's mediator in Israel/Palestine; and Wesley Clark, who commanded NATO forces in the Kosovo operation. They all say that it will not be militarily easy, that it is not militarily necessary at this time, and that it will have negative consequences for the United States. It is believed that these retired military leaders speak for many who are still serving.

Two more who have spoken out are Richard Armey, the Republican majority leader in the House, and Senator Chuck Hagel, Vietnam veteran and Republican senator from Nebraska. This adds up to powerful internal opposition to the proposed Bush adventure. Note that there are no Democrats on this list. The Democrats have been extraordinarily and shamefully timid throughout the debate.

Then there is the opposition from the friends and allies of the United States. The Canadians say they haven't seen the evidence that would justify an invasion. The Germans say they definitely won't send troops. The Russians have spent the last several weeks having very ostentatious discussions with all three members of the "axis of evil"—Iraq, Iran, and North Korea. The "moderate" Arab countries are falling over each other to be the first to say that they won't allow their territory to be used for an attack on Iraq: Saudi Arabia, Jordan, Egypt, Bahrain, Qatar. The Kurds refused to come to a meeting of the Iraqi opposition held under U.S. auspices in the U.S. And even with Great Britain, the U.S. is running into trouble. Yes, Tony Blair seems unflaggingly loyal, although he is complaining that the U.S. is not giving him anything to help him (that is, concrete evidence that he can show others). A majority of British citizens are opposed to military action, and Blair refuses to allow a discussion in the British cabinet because he knows of strong opposition there, above all from Robin Cook.

Yes, George W. Bush does have staunch supporters— Ariel Sharon and Tom DeLay. But that's about it. What does the U.S. administration say in response to the criticisms? Bush himself belittles the debate as a "frenzy" and says that no decision has yet been made, which no one believes. Vice-President Cheney says that, even if Saddam Hussein were now to accept the return of inspectors, he should still be overthrown (a position that even Tony Blair finds unacceptable). And Secretary of Defense Rumsfeld says that when the U.S. decides what is right to do, and does it, others will follow. This, he says, is what we mean by leadership.

The point is that, from the perspective of the hawks, which now includes George W. Bush himself, opposition is irrelevant. They are actually happier to go ahead without anyone else pitching in to help. What they wish to demonstrate is that no one can defy the U.S.

government and get away with it. They wish to overthrow Saddam Hussein, no matter what he does or others say, because Saddam Hussein has thumbed his nose at the United States. The hawks believe that it is only by crushing Saddam that they can persuade the rest of the world that the U.S. is top dog and should be obeyed in every way. That is why they are also pushing the mad idea of getting other countries to sign bilateral agreements with the United States, guaranteeing special treatment for U.S. citizens in matters within the purview of the newly established International Criminal Court. The principle here is the same. The U.S. cannot be subject to international law, for it is top dog.

Of course, what all the opposition is saying—the friendly opposition, not that of al-Qaeda—is that the United States is shooting itself in the foot and, in the process, is going to cause enormous damage to everyone else. Aside from the fact that the proposed action is illegal under international law (invading a country is aggression, and aggression is a war crime), it is foolish. Let us look at the three possible outcomes of an invasion. The U.S. may win swiftly and easily, with minimal loss of life. The U.S. may win after a long, exhausting war, with considerable loss of life. The U.S. may lose, as in Vietnam, and may be forced to withdraw from Iraq after considerable loss of life. Swift and easy victory, obviously the hope of the U.S. administration, is the least likely. I give it one chance in twenty. Winning after a long exhausting war is the most likely, perhaps two chances out of three. And actually losing, incredible as it seems (but then it seemed so in Vietnam too), is a plausible outcome, one chance in three.

Any of these three outcomes will damage the national interests of the United States. Suppose the U.S. wins easily and rapidly. It will impress the entire world, intimidate the entire world, and scare the living daylights out of the entire world. Nothing will guarantee a more rapid loss of real political influence in the world—above all, among our allies and friends—than this outcome so desired by the hawks in the U.S. government. The hawks argue that it will restore U.S. power. In fact, it will devastate it. We will be friendless; except for a few sycophants, the vast majority of countries will be seething with resentment.

And then there's the problem of what we do next after the easy victory. We have promised Turkey and Jordan and probably Saudi Arabia that we will not allow Iraq to disintegrate. But can we keep that promise? Yes, if we send in a U.S. proconsul and at least 200,000 troops for long-term occupation of the country (as in Japan after 1945). But we have no intention of doing this, and the idea would have very negative consequences for the U.S. administration at home. A post-invasion Iraq would be something like Bosnia in the early 1990s— prey to internal and external ethnicizing forces. And the U.S. can't decide if it wants Iran on its side or wishes to invade that country next. In any case, Iran will take every advantage of a defeated Iraq that it can, and would indeed welcome the latter's disintegration.

The so-called moderate Arab states have been screaming that a U.S. invasion will hurt first of all their regimes, which may not survive, and will make virtually impossible what is already remote, namely any settlement in Israel/Palestine. This seems so obvious that one wonders how the U.S. administration can have any doubts about it. Both the Israeli and the Palestinian hawks will be infinitely strengthened, and less ready than ever to consider any arrangements, no matter who proposes them.

Then there is the most probable outcome—a long, drawn-out, bloody war. Iraq may well be "bombed into the stone age," as impetuous hawks often dream. It may even be "nuked into the stone age." In the process, Iraq will launch whatever terrible weapons it has. These may be less numerous and powerful than U.S. propaganda asserts, but even a few such weapons could wreak immense human damage all over the region (including of course in Israel, above all). The body bags will give rise to envenomed civil strife in the U.S. The economic costs of warfare, as well as its impact on the world's oil supply, will do the same kind of long-term damage to the U.S.'s relative position in the world-economy as did the Vietnam War. And if we are saddled with the moral blame of adding new nuclear bombings to those of Hiroshima and Nagasaki, it may take fifty years to calm world opinion. And then, when we've finally won, we'll have the same problem of what to do next and even less inclination to do it.

The third possible outcome—defeat—is so awesome that one hesitates to think how future generations will judge it. They will probably blame most the inability of anybody in Washington to reflect on this as a serious possibility. The psychiatrists call this denial.

Could Osama bin Laden ask for more?

September 15, 2002: "*9/11, One Year Later*"

Everyone knows today to what the symbol "9/11" refers. It refers to the day on which a group of followers of Osama bin Laden seized control of four airplanes in the United States and managed to destroy the Twin Towers in New York and damage the Pentagon outside Washington. Several thousand persons lost their lives. As a result, President Bush declared a "war on terrorism," which, he said, "we will certainly win." He called on everyone everywhere to support the U.S. in this war, and said that those who were not with us were against us. He promised to capture Osama bin Laden, "dead or alive."

The American people's immediate reaction to the attack was one of very large-scale support for President Bush and what he proposed to do. In addition, there was a wave of worldwide sympathy for America under attack. To the astonishment of many, the editorial in *Le Monde* the next day was entitled "We are all Americans now." Bush's initial mode of implementing his program was twofold: Internationally, he sought to create a wide coalition of anti-terrorist activities, including the sending of troops to Afghanistan to overthrow the Taliban regime and to destroy al-Qaeda, thought to be located largely within Afghanistan. Internally, he sought to improve considerably measures of security, most notably by the passage of the Patriot Act, which gave unprecedented powers to the U.S. government in overcoming legal obstacles to its activities. This act passed the U.S. Congress almost unanimously.

The initial success of the Bush policies thus appeared to be considerable. The United States seemed to hold the high ground in world public opinion. The Taliban were removed militarily from power without too much difficulty. And although neither bin Laden nor most of the al-Qaeda leadership were captured, they seemed to be "on the run." Then the situation began to change. First of all, the United States shifted the locus of its attention. The pursuit of bin Laden and al-Qaeda seemed to fade into the background and to be replaced by a different objective, "regime change" in Iraq. This objective did not get the worldwide assent that the "war on terrorism" evoked. Quite the contrary. So many voices seemed to rise up in protest against "preemptive action" that the U.S. government is now working full time to make sure that it is not totally isolated on this issue. *Le Monde* ran a second editorial one year later, in which it said: "The reflex of solidarity of one year ago has been transformed into a wave that might lead one to believe that, across the world, we have all become anti-Americans." The chancellor of Germany, a country only a year ago still thought to be an indefatigable ally of the United States, is gaining in public opinion in a close electoral battle precisely because he has asserted that Germany will not send troops to invade Iraq, even if the Security Council authorizes it.

What happened during this year? The answer depends on who you ask. Let us start with those who are called the hawks in the U.S. administration, and who now seem to call the tune. They will say that they have cut through the wishy-washy support upon which the U.S. has long relied, and are asserting—for the first time in over fifty years—the only kind of policy that will guarantee the national interests of the United States. They assert that the U.S. has not only the right to engage in preemptive action but the moral duty to do so. They know that this stance discomforts many people and many governments. But they believe, as Secretary Rumsfeld said last week, that if the United States decides something is right to do and then does it, others will see that it was right and will eventually support it. Unilateralism, for the hawks, is neither wrong nor imprudent; on the contrary, it is the path of wisdom.

Which others is Rumsfeld talking about? He is talking about all those who, claiming to share U.S. values, hesitate at the image of unilateralism and urge a return to "multilateralism": in the United States, Republican stalwarts like James Baker, as well as the Clintonites; elsewhere, the people of Canada and Western Europe (which are the traditional allies of the United States) as well as the so-called moderates in the Islamic world. Rumsfeld feels their objections are all puff, and when the dragon emits his flames, they will all crumble. Is Rumsfeld right about how they will act when they are largely ignored? We shall see, although he is probably right in part. Some of them are already crumbling, and are merely asking for a façade of consultation so that they may then assent.

If you asked the moderates in the Islamic world, they would seem to be shaking their heads over the madness of the hawks. They live daily in touch with their local reality. They know the limits of their own power. They know also, better than the United States, the limits of U.S. power in their region. For them, it is a bit like Samson pulling down the temple. They are under the roof and will be crushed as well. But they also know that their voices amount to little in Washington today. No doubt many of them are putting their personal fates in the hands of Allah and perhaps some Swiss bankers as well.

If you asked bin Laden what has been happening, he would probably say, were he able to talk the cynical language of the geopoliticians, that all is going according to plan. President Bush says that the U.S. objective is to strengthen the prospects of democracy in the Middle East. But that dedicated minority of persons who truly have this as an objective are wringing their hands in desperation. They know that no viable democratic regimes are going to emerge from this next explosion in the Middle East. They can only expect fanatic Islamists and repressive generals, thus eliminating the few pockets of space these persons now have. Torture, not liberty, awaits them.

Saddam Hussein is a nasty fellow. But he has been that for a long, long time, and for most of this time has had the strong support of the U.S., Soviet/Russian, and French governments. He is, when all is said and done, a very minor figure on the world scene, and furthermore historically a rather prudent figure. His primary goal is to remain in power. His secondary goal is to strengthen the Arab world militarily, with him as the leader—and this is exactly what has made him prudent.

The dangers that the coming Iraqi war pose for all of us are threefold: (1) It may go far toward creating Huntington's "clash of civilizations," transforming it from a rhetorical misapprehension of reality into an organizing principle. (2) It will probably lead to the use of nuclear weapons, thereby ending the taboo and making their use commonplace in the future. (3) It will legitimate "preemptive action," something the interstate system has been trying to outlaw for some 500 years. And on top of all of this, there will be no clear-cut outcome, no immediate end in sight. We live in·a chaotic world. But we don't have to up the ante so radically. Unfortunately, we are going to.

October 1, 2002: *"The Battle of the Resolutions"*

The second U.S.-Iraqi war is undergoing its mobilizing skirmishes. It is the battle of the resolutions—two resolutions to be specific, one to be passed by the U.S. Congress and one to be passed by the U.N. Security Council.

The story starts somewhere in the early summer of 2002. At that time, the decision of the U.S. government to invade Iraq soon had clearly been taken. The hawks believed they had won entirely the internal U.S. battle. What they wanted was an invasion in October, *without* any resolutions. They didn't want resolutions for two reasons. They thought they might have some difficulty in getting the kind of resolutions they would find acceptable. But even more important, they wanted to show that they didn't need the resolutions, now or in the future. They wished to establish the principle that the U.S. government could and would engage in preemptive action anywhere at any time if they thought it desirable. And they wished to start the war in October to guarantee a Republican majority in both houses of Congress in the November elections.

To its surprise, the U.S. government ran into more opposition than it had expected—not only from the dubious allies (France, Russia, China, Saudi Arabia, Egypt, U.S. Democrats) but also from more influential sources: the so-called old Bushies (that is, high-ranking Republican personalities); Representative Armey, the Republican majority leader in the House; and a long list of very prominent retired generals (obviously speaking for the Army generals on active duty). In addition, Tony Blair explained that he was having a hard time pulling along the British public and British politicians. The pivotal figure, President Bush himself, decided that he would have to stanch the outflow of support, and that the way to do this was by seeking the resolutions. The main internal arguments were threefold: (1) The U.S. government could get the resolutions; (2) Saddam Hussein would never agree to real inspections; and (3) the U.S. could then start the war in January, but with greater international and national support. January seems to be a deadline imposed by the U.S. military because of climate conditions in Iraq. If not January, then a postponement of at least six to nine months beyond January. Furthermore, the fight for the resolutions, by putting the fire under the feet of the Democrats, would serve almost as well politically in November as an actual war.

So, in September, Bush made his speech to the United Nations, and called for the two sets of resolutions (U.N.

and U.S. Congress). This decision was actually a minor victory for the Powell/Army generals/"old Bushies" faction. That they were pleased and appeased can be noticed in the congratulatory op-ed piece that James A. Baker wrote immediately. That the hawks were less than pleased can be read in great detail in the article published just before the speech in the September issue of *Commentary* magazine by that old superhawk, Norman Podhoretz. The article is entitled "In Praise of the Bush Doctrine." It is a fascinating article and is worth reading carefully. It makes three points: (1) The Bush doctrine of preemptive action is terrific and is in the tradition of Ronald Reagan and *not* of Bush's father; (2) Bush (junior) has been good on these issues only since 9/11; (3) Bush seems to be wobbling now. The key sentence, in good American colloquial style, is: "That is not to say that the count is in yet whether Bush will walk the walk as well as he has talked the talk."

What Podhoretz has in mind in "walking the walk" is that, after Afghanistan and Iraq, Bush should take on not only Iran and North Korea but Syria, Lebanon, Libya, and then Saudi Arabia, Egypt, and the Palestinian Authority (even without Arafat). Podhoretz exempts Pakistan only because of the turnaround of Musharref, but if Musharref were to go, clearly Podhoretz would add Pakistan to the list. So, at least we know that the hawks are thinking of absolutely continuous warfare in the Muslim world (and no doubt beyond—Cuba anyone?).

Now what I can read, members of the U.S. Congress and of the U.N. Security Council can read as well. Will they then pass the resolutions? Yes, of course, but that is not the battle. The battle is in the wording of the resolutions. And the battle is in how the battle is being fought.

In the U.S. Congress, the battle is being fought with a mix of intimidation and weaseling. The Bush camp is

threatening the Democrats with a charge of appease-
ment or worse if they don't vote the resolution in the
form the government wants. This has clearly worked,
up to a point. The Democratic leadership have been
anxious to agree on a resolution swiftly so that they can
try to use the remaining time before the election to remind voters of other issues (the state of the economy,
threats to social security, insurance for seniors needing
medical prescriptions, etc.). But there is a lot of unease
about the war out there among ordinary voters. Al Gore
decided to stake his renewed campaign for the presidency by issuing a note of great caution about Iraq. He
is being viciously denounced for this. Nonetheless, the
speech was enough to encourage Senator Kennedy (and
others) to echo it, to get Tom Daschle to express public
anger at Bush's attack on the Democrats' asserted lack of
"concern for national security," and to encourage Representative Bonior, No. 2 Democrat in the House, to fly off
to Baghdad and to say, Let's not rush to war yet. The
result of all of this is that the original proposed resolution has been watered down slightly. It now will give
Bush sanction not for any and all military actions but
only for one in Iraq. That version will probably pass by
very large majorities in a week or so, although there still
may be wrangling over the wording.

The debate in the U.N. Security Council is probably
more difficult for Bush. The U.S. wants a tight deadline
on Iraqi disarmament and an authorization for war if
that doesn't occur. Iraq has confounded Bush by saying
it will accept inspectors, but apparently only on the basis of the last (1998) U.N. resolution that the U.S. finds
far below the acceptable norm. Hans Blix, on behalf of
the United Nations, is in Vienna right now, negotiating
for a return of inspectors, but of course on the basis of
the existing U.N. mandate, that of 1998.

Meanwhile, the U.S. has been putting great pressure on the three doubtful veto-holding members—France, Russia, and China—to get them to accept (or at least not to veto) what the British will propose (which is what the U.S. wants). So far, each of the three has issued statements that are ambivalent. France has said that it absolutely does not want an authorization for war in the resolution, that such an authorization should be in a second, later resolution, once it is determined that Iraq has defied the first resolution. The French version would put off the war for a while, on the grounds that it will not only take time to determine whether the first resolution was defied but also require agreement that this was the case. Therefore, a second resolution formula would move us beyond January, and into the fall of 2003. France, Russia, and China will have an eye on one another, and will probably in some sense synchronize their final positions. We cannot be sure of the wording of a U.N. resolution at this point. But even with enormous U.S. arm-twisting, it is probable that the U.N. resolution will be weaker than the U.S. wants.

So, what may we expect? A fairly strong U.S. Congress resolution, uncertain electoral results in November, and an in-between U.N. resolution. And then ambiguous responses by Saddam Hussein to whatever the U.N. tries to do. Come December, we shall be at the moment of choice. The world will not agree on whether Hussein is fulfilling the U.N. resolution. And we are back to the issue of whether the U.S. proceeds alone (probably with Great Britain). For the hawks, it would be now or never. And they will push their hardest to go ahead in January, with or without international sanction. President Bush will either be their hero or their villain. I would bet he prefers to be their hero, whatever the longer-term consequences.

October 15, 2002: "*The U.S.-Iraqi War, Seen from the Longue Durée*"

What can be said about a U.S.-Iraqi war, seen from the *longue durée*? Three things principally. The first has to do with the reasons for which the United States is taking the position it is taking at the moment. We have to think of the United States as a hegemonic power in the world-system, in the beginning phase of its decline. Its rise began approximately in 1873, when the U.S. positioned itself as one of two possible successor powers (the other being Germany) to the United Kingdom, which had passed its peak and was beginning its decline as the hegemonic power.

The long ascent of the United States took place from 1873 to 1945, and required defeating Germany in a long "thirty years' war" that went from 1914 to 1945. This was followed by its brief moment of true hegemony, from 1945 to 1970. During this period, the United States was by far the most efficient producer on the world economic scene. It dominated the world politically, via a status quo accord with its only military rival, the U.S.S.R. (an accord to which we refer metaphorically as the Yalta arrangements), and a series of politico-military alliances (NATO, the U.S.-Japan Defense Treaty, ANZUS), which guaranteed to the U.S. the automatic military and political support of a series of major industrial powers. This hegemony was sustained by a U.S. military machine based on air power and nuclear weapons (combined with a "balance of terror" with the Soviet Union).

These halcyon conditions were disturbed by two things primarily. The first was the economic rise of Western Europe and Japan in the 1960s, which ended the overwhelming economic superiority of the United States and transformed the world-system into a roughly equal

triadic economic structure. The second was the unwillingness of certain countries of the Third World—especially China, Vietnam, and Cuba—to accept the
implications of the U.S.–Soviet Union status quo agreements.

The combination of the beginning of a Kondratieff
B-phase (largely the consequence of the economic rise of
Western Europe and Japan, and therefore of declining
monopolistic profits), the war in Vietnam (which also
led to delinking the U.S. dollar from gold, and which
ended in defeat), and the world revolution of 1968 (which
among other things undermined the legitimacy of the
Yalta arrangements) marked the beginning of the end of
the U.S.'s ability to enforce its version of world order in
the geopolitical arena.

The story of the United States from 1970 to today is
the story of a battle to slow down geopolitical decline
amidst a worldwide economic stagnation: the Trilateral
Commission and the G-7 (as ways to induce Western
Europe and Japan not to move away from U.S. control
too fast), the Washington Consensus and neo-liberalism
(as ways to hold back the surge forward of the South),
and anti-proliferation as a doctrine (as a way to push off
inevitable military decline). If one wishes to take the
measure of all these efforts, one would have to say that
they were at best partially successful. They did reduce
the speed of the decline but did not stop it from occurring, with the United States all the while denying that it
was occurring.

Enter the hawks! The hawks in the United States
were never in political power from 1941 to 2001. They
chafed. After 9/11, they finally seized the reins of power
in Washington. Their view of the world is that decline is
real, but that its cause is the weak will and misguided
policies of the U.S. government (all U.S. governments

from Roosevelt to the present president before 9/11). They believe that U.S. potential power is unbeatable provided only that it is exercised. They are not unilateralists by default, but unilateralists by preference. They believe that unilateralism is itself a demonstration of power and a reinforcement of power.

The second thing that is going on is the North-South struggle, which will be a major focus of world conflict in the next twenty-five to fifty years. From the viewpoint of the South, there are several different ways of conducting this struggle. One mode is military-confrontational. That is the path that Saddam Hussein has chosen. The reasoning that lies behind this position is Bismarckian. Only if the South achieves greater political unity and greater real military strength will it be able to get its fair share of the world's resources. Its geopolitical strategy should be built around these premises. Hence, Saddam Hussein has always pushed for greater Arab unification (around him as leader, to be sure) and for obtaining so-called weapons of mass destruction. Ergo, everything the hawks say about him is true, except for one thing: that he is reckless, and likely to use such weapons readily. Quite the contrary. He has shown himself to be a relatively prudent, careful chess player, but one willing to make bold moves (and then retreat, if they prove to be mistakes or get him into a blocked position).

Personally, I find him an extremely terrible dictator, and I do not trust his virtue. But I see no reason to believe that he would use weapons of mass destruction more readily or recklessly than the United States or Israel (or any other power that has them, for that matter). I certainly do not believe that proliferation is stoppable in the middle run. And I am not at all sure that the world would be more peaceful if it were to be stopped. The fact that the Soviet Union had the hydrogen bomb explained, in large part, why the cold war was cold. We have gone from one to eight known possessors of nuclear weapons between 1945 and today, and there will be twenty more in the next twenty-five years. Iraq will be one of them, with or without Saddam Hussein.

The third structural trend to take into account in evaluating the present situation is the economic rise and geopolitical hesitations of Western Europe and Japan. No longer economically dependent on the United States, increasingly chafing at U.S. unilateralism, and uncomfortable about U.S. cultural arrogance, Western Europe and Japan remain hesitant to engage in actions that would deeply offend the United States. So their role on the world scene now is one of considerable timidity—on almost all issues. This is partly the heritage of cold war gratitudes, partly the result of sharing some geopolitical interests as a component of the North, partly a generational issue (the younger are less timid). This hesitancy will not last. By 2010, it will have disappeared completely. But for the moment, it still operates and explains current positions.

Putting together these three realities—the fact that the hawks are not open to persuasion, the fact that the South is indeed seeking to strengthen itself militarily, and the fact that Western Europe and Japan are not willing yet to be full actors on the scene—will enable anyone to analyze and even predict the immediately likely (and increasingly unpleasant) occurrences on the current world scene.

November 15, 2002: "*Bush: Fear Conquered Hope*"

Mr. Bush had his way—in the U.S. elections, in the U.N. Security Council. With Lula's victory in Brazil, hope conquered fear. With Bush's victory, fear conquered hope. There is much satisfaction now among the people in Mr. Bush's administration. They think they can get their program fully carried out. They are counting on a Congress and a Security Council that will continue to follow the Bush agenda. They think they have Saddam Hussein cornered.

What is their agenda? The interesting thing to note is that they have a short-term agenda and a long-term agenda, but absolutely no middle-term agenda. Their short-term agenda within the United States is to satisfy their three constituencies—the economic conservatives, the social conservatives, and the macho militarists. The economic conservatives are interested primarily in two things: lower taxes and reduction of the constraints that environmentalist considerations have put on them. The social conservatives are interested in legislating sexuality, harsher penalties for lawbreakers, and freedom to own and use guns. The macho militarists are interested in enhancing U.S. military power and using it.

These short-term objectives can be implemented by making the tax cuts permanent, ending the estate tax, appointing right-wing judges to the federal courts, and invading Iraq. Now that they have the power to do these things, they will do them. The one thing that can be said about Bush's people is that they don't waffle. They make only the concessions they absolutely have to make; otherwise, they bulldoze their way through all the forests. No doubt there will be a few obstacles in their way—an occasional difficulty with the Congress (a Senate filibuster or two, a few "moderate" Republicans who hesitate to go all the way on particular bills), an attempt by other countries to interpret Saddam Hussein's future actions less dyspeptically than the version we shall hear from Condoleeza Rice. But the Bush administration's response to obstacles is brutal action to overcome them. And since it seemed to have worked this November, the administration has no incentive to mend its manners.

But why did it work? It seems clear that the overwhelming answer is fear—the fear felt by the American people, and by the rest of the world. September 11 shook up the American people. But if it did so, it is because they were already anxious, and September 11 simply crystallized a vague sentiment into a pressing concern. The American people are afraid of terrorists; they are afraid of Moslems; they are afraid of strangers. It is a fear that the U.S. is no longer as strong as it once was, is no longer as respected as it once was, is no longer as appreciated as it once was. It is a fear that the American standard of living is in danger—a fear of inflation and of deflation, a fear of losing employment, a fear that, as they live longer, they no longer live as well, because the health care for the older part of the population is far weaker than people expect and want. President Bush responds to that fear not by saying there is no problem, but by saying that there is a problem to which he has a remedy—tough, determined action. The Bush administration exudes confidence in itself and this attracts fearful people, enough at least who give their vote to toughness.

Of course, none of this explains how the U.S. got a 15–0 vote in the Security Council for its resolution—one that was undoubtedly a bit watered down but nonetheless permits the U.S. to proceed and, in due time, to invade Iraq. What accounts for this vote is also fear. But it is not Saddam Hussein who inspired this fear. There is not a single member of the Security Council who, in the absence of the drive by the U.S., would have brought this issue to the table. There is not a single member who really believes that Saddam Hussein poses a short-term threat to the peace of the world, or who thinks that action against Iraq is a priority concern of the world community.

So why, in the end, did they all vote for the resolution—even France, Russia, and China, even Syria? The answer is very simple. They are all afraid of the Bush administration. This administration has made it very clear that it will take whatever punitive action it can against any country that gets in its way—not merely Mauritius or Syria, but Germany and Canada. So each member of the Security Council has had to weigh the short-term consequences of defiance. And the price seemed high. Thus, although they wiggled, and got some (not too many) face-saving concessions, in the end they buckled. There was once a time when the friends and allies of the U.S. lined up happily behind U.S. leadership in a world crisis. That time is over. Now they line up unhappily because they are afraid, not of the U.S. in the abstract but of the Bush administration concretely.

One thing that has made this possible has been the worldwide collapse of the reformist center. There is a remarkable parallel, largely unnoticed in the press, between the last French elections and the last U.S. elections. The initial expectation was that the Socialists would win in France. The initial expectation was that the Democrats would win in the U.S. They both lost the crucial subvote by a very narrow margin. Le Pen edged out Jospin for second place in the first round by a tiny difference. A shift of 50,000 votes in two states of the U.S. would have given the Democrats control of the U.S. Senate.

There was a factor in common between the two defeats—the exhaustion of the historic program of the two parties. In both countries, large numbers of voters said that the party no longer stood for anything, that it was trying to imitate the conservatives, while losing its base. This is a reflection of the long-standing decline of the traditional center-left movements, which once dominated the world scene. Following the elections, both parties lack a clear leader and a clear program. They are beset by internal debates about whether they should move further to the center (and try to whittle away votes from the conservatives) or move to the left (and try to recoup the votes of the disillusioned). It is not an easy choice tactically, because either option will lose as well as gain votes. And neither tactic will work if there is no clear program. But will there be?

So, in the short run, the Bush agenda seems likely to prevail. In the long run, the Bush administration knows, too, what it wants—few restraints on the acquisition of wealth (no matter how much this results in national and world economic and social polarization); a rollback on the liberal social mores that have been enveloping the world scene; and de facto authoritarian structures, which define democracy as making minor choices among elite groups every few years.

But can the Bush administration get from the short-term agenda to the long-term agenda? It simply assumes that it can; it doesn't waste time thinking about the middle term. This is its Achilles heel. Can it really contain the havoc the Iraq invasion will cause in Middle East politics? Are average Americans really ready to devote the lives of their children and their money to Bush's agenda, especially if it doesn't pay off in security and prosperity, which it is unlikely to do? Can the dollar really stand the additional strain on its credibility? Can the U.S. really block nuclear proliferation? Can it really hold in check the populist upsurge that is occurring in Latin America? How soon will China, Japan, and Korea come to terms with one another in ways that the U.S. won't like?

The aggressive opening chess moves of the Bush administration have been spectacular. But have they been wise, even from its point of view? Can fear really triumph over hope for very long?

December 1, 2002: "Aciu! *Bush Fiddles While Rome Burns*"

Aciu is the Lithuanian word for "thank you." This is what the crowd in Vilnius shouted when President Bush addressed them, saying that now that Lithuania had joined NATO, an attack on Lithuania would be considered an attack on the United States. The president was very pleased. He said, thank you. The United States and President Bush are popular in east-central Europe. This is about the last region of the world, other than Israel, where Bush can be assured of such a reception today. So he bathed in the cheers of this friendly zone. But like Nero, he was fiddling while Rome was burning. The United States is burning, and President Bush seems completely unaware of this. So, unfortunately, do most Americans. Like Nero, Bush is sure that he can do what he wants, and this arrogant naiveté makes him blind to the political realities of the world and the nature of the real alternatives that any American president has in the twenty-first century. Bush thinks this is the age of the American empire and savors it. The world left does not help clarity in agreeing that this is indeed the age of the American empire, even if they denounce it. A world in political chaos is not an imperial world. And we would all do well to absorb this elementary fact into our consciousness.

The massive misperception of reality will only increase the level of damage and suffering that will be the consequence of this chaos from which no one, least of all the United States, will benefit. Bush is about to lead the United States into a war with Iraq, and he will do so even if the U.N. inspectors find nothing of significance to report. Richard Perle recently told a group of U.K. Labour Party M.P.s that the fact that U.N. inspectors would find nothing would be politically meaningless, since the U.S. already knows that Saddam Hussein is violating the U.N. resolution and will act on its knowledge. The M.P.s were said to have been shocked. The groundwork is being laid for the denigration of the U.N. effort. The press these days is full of long explanations by members of the Bush administration and their media acolytes as to why the head of the U.N.'s inspection efforts, Hans Blix, is programmed to find nothing, which therefore means that he and his team can be ignored (and no doubt will be).

The U.S. press is also full of attacks on Saudi Arabia—by members of the U.S. Congress, the press, and pundits—for not having decided to support unreservedly the attack on Iraq (as well as for parallel sins in the past). This is said to be embarrassing for President Bush, who is apparently still hoping to be able to twist the arms of the Saudis into at least passive cooperation with the invasion of Iraq. This political attack on the Saudis, however, is being orchestrated by the right wing of the right wing, which is seeking not Saudi Arabia's cooperation but Saudi Arabia's destruction. Who knows? It may succeed.

Meanwhile, Osama bin Laden has not been exactly inactive. There have been two major attacks on Western soft targets, in Bali and in Mombasa—both of which are probably his doing, or that of his allies. And he has released a long letter to the American people, which *The Observer* (London) published in English on November 24. It doesn't tell us anything new. What is striking about the long letter is its total militancy and its clarity of detail about a whole series of political issues around the globe. It is not illiterate screech. He has made complaints about Israel the centerpiece of this letter, which was not true of his previous letter, but he does not neglect other issues. The United States clearly has an intelligent enemy, who denounces the U.S. repeatedly for its double standards.

In terms of world geopolitics, the world has seen three major national elections in the second half of 2002: in Germany, the United States, and Brazil. Yes, Bush won the U.S. but he lost Germany and Brazil. There is a fourth key election coming up very soon—in South Korea. That election is now said to be close. A defeat for Bush there would not be a source of joy in the White House. Bush even lost a less important, but still meaningful, election—in Ecuador. There a populist soldier, Colonel Lucio Gutiérrez, defeated a super neo-liberal opponent. What is significant about this is not merely that the victor's rhetoric was populist, but that Gutiérrez is someone with partially *indio* ancestry, and he was supported by the strongest federation of indigenous organizations in the Americas, CONAIE. He is a hero of the failed attempt of these same forces to come to power in a coup two years ago. Now he was elected by a clear majority. It is true that Gutiérrez is speaking a cautious language on economic issues, but he will be an ally of Lula and not of Bush in the coming debates on a pan-American free trade zone (FTAA/ALCA). And he will be a voice for compromise and peace in Colombia, a development the Bush administration and the current president of Colombia are doing everything in their power to keep from happening.

Bush faces a difficult war in Iraq; a collapsing façade of pro-American "moderate" regimes in the Middle East; a very uncertain world-economy, which will be made worse by the Iraq adventure; populism in the Americas;

an ever-stronger China combined with a general recalci-
trance in Northeast Asia (that is, Japan, South Korea,
and China) against supporting the tough line on North
Korea that the Bush administration espouses. But all of
this is almost minor in its consequences for the United
States in comparison with the determined efforts of the
U.S. to isolate itself from its hitherto closest friends. Bush
won't invite the prime minister of Canada to his ranch,
and remains frigid toward the chancellor of Germany.
This is because neither thinks it's a terribly smart idea to
invade Iraq. And there are many in the Bush administration who think that Bush's response to the heresy of
these two leaders has been much too mild. They argue
that these so-called closest allies of the United States are
unreliable, foolish, even cowardly, and certainly wrong
(about almost everything). They feel that Western Europe and Canada should be put in their place. They may
soon add Japan and South Korea to the list of school-
boys to reprimand and, if necessary, punish.

They have written off NATO because they can't count
on it to do their bidding. The east-central Europeans
may be celebrating their entry into NATO, feeling that
they will thereby get closer to the U.S. They will soon
learn that the U.S. is in the process of scuttling NATO
by making it irrelevant to world politics. But can the
United States even survive in today's world, much less
do well, without the strong support of those who have
been its closest allies in the past fifty years? I doubt it
very much. Rome is burning, and Bush is fiddling.

December 15, 2002: *"The Politics of Multilateralism"*

As we know, the Bush administration has been divided
between what we may call the "unilateralists" (presum-

ably led by Rumsfeld and Cheney) and the "multilateralists" (presumably led by Colin Powell). We now know
that immediately on September 12, 2001, Rumsfeld rec-
ommended war on Iraq as a response to the al-Qaeda
attacks. Of course, in 2000, before they took office, he
and Cheney had been signatories of a document calling
for the overthrow of Saddam Hussein. These people
wished not only to end Iraq's possession of weapons of
mass destruction but also to change the regime and, indeed, occupy the country. Furthermore, they wished on
principle to do this unilaterally, without asking anyone's
permission.

As we also know, they ran into a lot of political objections from important sources—the secretary of state,
the so-called old Bushies (close to the president's father),
Tony Blair, and some Republican senators. All of them
argued that the same objective could be achieved via
"multilateral" action, and without the negative political
fallout in which a "unilateral" action would result. This
led to the multilateral resolutions—one in the U.S. Congress and one in the U.N. Security Council. Both resolutions gave the Bush administration a green light for what
they wanted to do, with some minor amendments and
the delay inherent in sending back the inspectors. But
what the Bush administration lost in slight delay it more
than gained in greater legitimization in the eyes of the
"multilateralists" around the world.

Multilateralism is the fig leaf that has made it possible for all sorts of "centrist" forces to say that they agreed
with the objective—ending Iraq's ability to employ weapons of mass destruction—without endorsing actions by
the U.S. that were "unilateral." But is multilateral action
to achieve the same end really better? What this sleight
of hand has done is to eliminate any real discussion of
the objective's legitimacy in the first place. Why should

the five permanent members of the Security Council— the U.S., Great Britain, France, Russia, and China—have the political and moral right to stock (and use) weapons of mass destruction but other presumably sovereign states not have this right?

If you press the question, the answer inevitably comes down to a moral judgment. The big five can be "trusted" with such weapons, which they would use only defensively. Other countries, particularly if they have regimes that are dictatorial *and* have foreign policies hostile to the United States, cannot be "trusted." Myself, I don't trust any government, and I mean *any* government, not to use such weapons if they thought it in their national interest to do so (which might mean just their national survival, but might also mean simply maintaining their overall standard of living).

The moral distinction between the trustworthy and the untrustworthy has been around throughout the history of the modern world-system. And it has always justified a doctrine of "interventionism" in which the "civilized" tame the barbarians. Going back to the sixteenth century, we have the famous debate between Las Casas, the Bishop of Chiapas, and Sepúlveda as to the moral rights of the Spaniards in their treatment of the Indians. One of Sepúlveda's key arguments was that the Spaniards had to intervene (militarily and religiously) in order to save innocent lives, which he believed were threatened by the barbaric practices of the Indians. The answer of Las Casas to this argument was that one could intervene to save human lives only if the process of saving them does not cause greater harm. And there we have the debate to this day.

In the nineteenth century, all sorts of European theoreticians justified the imposition of colonial rule in Asia and Africa on the grounds that they were thereby ending barbaric practices (for example, slavery, which these same Europeans had been practicing until a short time before; or alleged cannibalism; or *suttee* in India). In the 1930s, the United States was split between the "isolationists" and the "interventionists"; the latter were those who wished to join actively in the fight against the Nazis. In the period after 1945, there were many who wished to "liberate" countries from Communist rule, others who wished to support liberation movements against colonial or racist powers, and, most recently, those who wished to intervene—in the Balkans, in Africa—to prevent "genocides."

I have run the gamut of varieties of interventionism to indicate that the moral issues are not simple ones. We all believe in interventionism in some instances and fight it in others. The modern world-system is however based on an anomaly. It enshrines on the one hand the so-called sovereign rights of all states, which logically and legally define all outside interventions as aggression and illegitimate, but also, on the other hand, the implicit natural-law argument that there exist overriding moral values underlying the world-system (which these days we are calling human rights) and that those who violate these values have no right to remain in power anywhere.

How then do we deal with this anomaly? Well, we can deal with it as a moral-philosophical problem to be debated. Or we can make clear judgments that imply real action in the political arena. In fact, not too many people spend time discussing the moral-political dilemmas. And the people who make clear judgments matter only if they have the power to carry them out. So, when these clear judgments are made by the Bush administration, they do what they are doing. And when these clear judgments are made by people in less powerful structures, these people are usually condemned to do nothing or, at most, to engage in trying to sabotage the actions of the powerful.

But the Las Casas principle—intervention to save lives is justified only if it doesn't cause more damage than it prevents—is a good guide to legitimate action in the world arena. And those who are supporting "multilateral" action to end what they perceive as the risk to human lives incarnated by Saddam Hussein's continuing to be in power and to have weapons of mass destruction ought to be asking themselves whether the "multilateral" action they are recommending meets the Las Casas standard. This is a moral and political decision that has to be based on a close reading of the present situation and the probable consequences of an invasion of Iraq.

When Tony Blair says, as he did a year ago or so, that inaction is not an option, one has to ask, and ask very seriously, Why not?

January 15, 2003: *"Can War Be Averted in Iraq?"*

The simple answer is no, because the U.S. hawks won't take anything the Iraqis say or do as an acceptable reason to call off the war dogs. I feel we are in the midst of the novel by Gabriel Garcia Márquez, *Chronicle of a Death Foretold*, a story of death as a social ritual. The United States is going to war with Iraq primarily in order to go to war with Iraq. It is for this reason that nothing that the inspectors say, nothing that the other members of the Security Council (including Great Britain) say, certainly nothing that Saddam Hussein may say, will make any difference.

The war with Iraq was publicly requested during the last years of the Clinton administration in a statement of some twenty hawks, including Cheney and Rumsfeld. We now know that within days of the September 11 attack, President Bush gave his imprimatur to such a war. All the rest has been pretense and maneuvering. The open defiance of the United States by North Korea in the last three months, and the evasive response to this defiance by the U.S. government, provides further evidence that the real issue is not Iraq's noncompliance with various U.N. resolutions.

So, why do Bush and the hawks feel that a war is essential? They reason in the following way. The United States is not doing so well these days. In the words of some analysts, the U.S. is in hegemonic decline. Its economy is in an uncertain state. Most of all, it cannot be sure that it will outcompete Western Europe and Japan/ East Asia in the decades to come. With the collapse of the Soviet Union, it has lost the major political argument it had to persuade Western Europe and Japan to follow all its political initiatives. All it has left is an extremely strong military.

Madeleine Albright, when she was secretary of state, became furious at one point at the reticence of some of the high-ranking military to endorse her view of what should be done in the Balkans, and is reported to have said, "What is the point of having the strongest military in the world, if we can never use it?" The hawks make that viewpoint the centerpiece of their analysis. They believe that the U.S. has the strongest military in the world, that the U.S. can win any military encounter it undertakes, and that U.S. prestige and power in the world-system can be restored only by a show of force. The point of the force is not to achieve regime change in Iraq (probably a minor benefit, considering what might replace the current regime). Rather, it is to intimidate the *allies* of the United States, so that they stop their carping, their criticisms, and fall back into line, meekly as the school-children they are considered to be by the hawks.

The Bush administration has not been divided between unilateralists and multilateralists. They are all unilateralists. Those we call "multilateralists" are simply those who have argued that the U.S. can get its position formally adopted by others (the U.N., NATO), and that, if such resolutions are adopted, the policy is that much easier to implement. The "multilateralists" have always said that, if they fail to get the votes in the U.N. or elsewhere that they need, the U.S. can always go it alone. And the so-called "unilateralists" have bought this line because of the reserve clause. The only difference between the two groups is their estimate of how likely it is to get others to support the U.S. line. What we have therefore is a multilateralism that takes this form: The U.S. is multilateral to the degree that others adopt the U.S. unilateral position; if not, not.

The basic problem is that the hawks really believe their own analysis. They believe that once the war in Iraq is won (and they tend to think this will be achieved relatively easily), everyone else will fall into line, the whole Middle East will be reconfigured to the desires of the U.S. hawks, Europe will shut up, and North Korea and Iran will tremble and therefore renounce all aspirations to weaponry.

The whole world is yelling at the U.S. that the situation is far more complicated than that, that a U.S. military invasion of Iraq will probably make the world situation worse, and that the hawks are reaping the whirlwind. They do not listen, because they do not believe that this is so. They are impressed with the power of the bully. It is called hubris.

The folly of this war that has been so abundantly foretold is that, in addition to causing untold and essentially unnecessary suffering for all sorts of people (and not only in Iraq), it will actually weaken the geopolitical position of the United States and diminish the legitimacy of any of its future positions on the world political scene. We are living in a truly chaotic world, and U.S. pretensions to an impossible "imperium" amount to increasing the speed of an automobile going downhill with brakes that are no longer functioning properly. It is suicidal, and not least for the United States itself.

February 1, 2003: *"France Is the Key"*

During the Second World War Winston Churchill said that the greatest cross he had to bear was the Cross of Lorraine (the symbol of Charles de Gaulle). After 1945, the United States came to feel that this had become its cross. France has consistently pursued a "Gaullist" foreign policy under all its postwar governments, whether led by de Gaulle, Gaullists, or anyone else. The essence of the Gaullist foreign policy is that France, while part and parcel of the "West," has asserted the right to its own views of how to achieve world order, and has insisted that the United States, as the most powerful Western country, has to take France's views into account. France, unlike any other of the allies of the United States, has always sought to refuse a "unilateralist" leadership by the U.S. in a meaningful way.

Over the past fifty years, the United States has tried everything it could to dissuade France from this attitude: sweet talk, forceful pressure, conspiracy, and huffing and puffing. Nothing the U.S. did seemed to change France's basic stance. When recently Donald Rumsfeld contemptuously dismissed "old Europe," it was France he had uppermost in mind. In the past, the United States has counted on Germany to moderate France's views, or at least not to go along with France. It is thus with enormous displeasure that the Bush administration has observed the Schroeder/Fischer turn in German foreign policy. The U.S. hawks feel betrayed.

So, it is particularly galling to the U.S. that today France is the key to whether or not the forthcoming U.S. invasion of Iraq will be considered "legitimate" by the majority of people in the Western world, and even beyond it. If France goes along with the U.S., however reluctantly, the war will widely be considered something sanctioned by the United Nations and therefore by that mysterious entity, the "world community." If France refuses to go along, it brings with itself not only Germany but Russia, China, Canada, and Mexico—a powerful lineup. Japan has let it be known that it will follow "world opinion," meaning quite obviously only if the U.S. can get U.N. cover.

France even determines the position of Great Britain. In *The Independent* of January 30, Donald Macintyre wrote an article with the headline "Blair is playing for high stakes, and he needs Chirac to come to his rescue." Macintyre discusses the difficulties Blair is having at home, namely the "threatened revolt" in the Labour Party, and says that whether it comes off or not depends on France's position. "It's not too glib to say that [Blair's] future may be decided not in the White House, nor in No. 10 [Downing Street, the residence of the British prime minister], but in the Elysée [Chirac's official residence]."

What gives France this power? It is certainly not France's moral rectitude. France is as willing as the United States to send troops to defend its interests. Its current intervention in the Côte d'Ivoire and its current difficulties there as a result of this intervention attest to France's continuing role as a mini-imperial power in

Africa. Nor is it because France is somehow anti-American in its inner soul. No doubt there is a good deal of anti-American sloganeering in France (but then there is also a good deal of anti-French sloganeering in the United States). Nevertheless, in general, the French (both elites and ordinary people) find much to appreciate in the United States, remember the U.S. role in the two World Wars with gratitude, and share most basic values and most basic prejudices with the United States.

What gives France this power is the sense, throughout the world, that the United States is often, as good American slang would have it, "too big for its britches." And this is especially true now that the hawks have taken over the U.S. government. France's resentment over this, France's desire to limit the effects of U.S. arrogance, is shared just about everywhere in the world, with very few exceptions. So when France resists U.S. pressures, as it is now doing, it is cheered on in private by all the governments that don't dare do the same or don't dare do it quite as loudly—like Egypt or Korea or Brazil, or indeed Canada.

Actually, the U.S. government is aware of France's political power. This is why Colin Powell was able to convince Bush to go the United Nations in the first place, and why the U.S. is coming back to the United Nations next week to present some "evidence" about Saddam Hussein. The U.S. doesn't believe that this "evidence" is what will convince anyone. Rather, it believes that presenting the evidence will give France the excuse to follow what the U.S. government thinks are France's economic interests. The reasoning of the U.S. administration, about which it talks in the press almost openly, is that France will say to itself the following: (1) The U.S. will go into Iraq no matter what. (2) The U.S. will win easily. (3) If France sends troops, however unimportant militarily, France will be allowed to participate in the division of the spoils (oil); but if France stays out, it will be excluded.

The U.S. hawks are thus making a "crude Marxist" analysis of France's foreign policy—a one-to-one short-term correlation between economic gain and political position. But crude Marxism never works, because nothing is one-to-one and the short term is, as Fernand Braudel said, "dust." The problem, seen from France's point of view, and more particularly from Chirac's point of view, is posed quite differently. First of all, French public opinion (like most of West European opinion) is very largely opposed to the war and highly skeptical of U.S. motives, both short term and long term. The French left has lined up solidly against the war. The extreme right, for other reasons, has done so as well. And the French conservative party in power, the UMP, is split down the middle between those who buy the U.S. argument and favor a "Blairite" foreign policy and those who remain "Gaullist" in spirit.

Chirac has therefore kept his options open. He has to weigh the political consequences internally. If he makes a mistake, it could have a long-term negative effect both on the future of his party, which he has just recently managed to consolidate into a powerful force, and on France's efforts to create a strong and independent Europe. Secondly, Chirac is not at all certain of a swift U.S. military victory. Too many military figures around the world are skeptical, and they probably include some of the top French military. Thirdly, Gaullism has worked thus far, and Gaullism has always involved a delicate balance. France does not want to cut itself off from the U.S. But for once, France is scarcely isolated in its resistance to U.S. action. This doesn't seem the moment to abandon a Gaullist stance.

The United States, as could be expected, is playing all its cards. It has lined up five of the present fifteen members of the European Union to say in a collective letter that they support the U.S. position. Of course, these five governments had already said the same in effect. But the joint letter is meant as pressure on France. In effect, the U.S. is trying to convince the French that if they don't go along, the U.S. will actively try to break up Europe. The U.S. also has a second threat in its arsenal. If France's "soft power" is its incarnation of a worldwide discomfiture with U.S. unilateralism, its "hard power" is its veto in the Security Council. So, the U.S. is saying that if the U.S. doesn't get the backing it wants from the United Nations, it will marginalize the role of the Security Council and thereby reduce France's "hard power." But of course the veto power of France is not of much use if France can never use it, for fear that the Security Council would become irrelevant.

The U.S. thinks France needs the U.S. badly. But it may well be the case that, in fact, the U.S. needs France badly. Whatever France's decision, the ultimate consequences may in part be determined by the actual war. A war easily won will tend to reward all those who went along with the U.S. A war that drags out will no doubt punish all those who went along with the U.S. However, a war unilaterally won, even if won quickly, may hurt as much as help the U.S. A war "multilaterally" won will do less damage to the U.S. position. Nelson Mandela has warned the U.S. that it is heading the world toward a holocaust. The hawks are absolutely deaf.

The fact is that, as a result of its Gaullism, France is the only country in the world today that can have any significant impact on the U.S. geopolitical position—not Great Britain, not Russia, not even China. This is not because France is so strong, but because it pushes consistently for a multipolar world and thereby incarnates a strong world force. The prospect that France would itself be a direct beneficiary of such a geopolitical transformation is far less important to most people in most countries than the prospect that France might succeed to some degree in creating something they all want. We shall soon know how France plays its cards. And the whole world will feel the difference.

February 15, 2003: "*The Righteous War*"

George Bush is about to lead the valiant troops into battle in righteous war against the despotic tyrant. He will not turn back, no matter what pusillanimous or venal European politicians, major religious figures around the world, retired generals, and other erstwhile friends of liberty and the U.S. may think or do. Never has a war had so much prior discussion and so little backing from world public opinion. No matter! The decision for war, based on a calculus of American power, was made in the White House a long time ago.

We have to ask ourselves why. To begin with, we have to lay to rest two major theories about the motivations of the U.S. government that have been insistently put forth. The first is that of those who favor the war. They argue that Saddam Hussein is a vicious tyrant who presents an imminent danger to world peace, and the earlier he is confronted the more likely he can be stopped from doing the damage he intends to do. The second theory is put forward primarily by opponents of the war. They argue that the U.S. is interested in controlling world oil. Iraq is a key element in the edifice. Overthrowing Hussein would put the U.S. in the driver's seat.

Neither thesis holds much water. Virtually everyone around the world agrees that Saddam Hussein is a vicious tyrant, but very few are persuaded he is an imminent danger to world peace. Most people regard him as a careful player of the geopolitical game. He is accumulating so-called weapons of mass destruction, to be sure. But it is doubtful that he would use them against anyone now for fear of the reprisals that would inevitably follow. He is certainly less likely, not more likely, to use them than North Korea. He is in a tight political corner and, were absolutely nothing done, he would probably be unable to move out of it. As for his links with al-Qaeda, the whole affair lacks credibility. He may play tactically and marginally with al-Qaeda, but not one-tenth as intensively as the U.S. government itself did for a long time. In any case, should al-Qaeda grow stronger, he is near the top of its list for liquidation as an apostate. These charges of the U.S. government are propaganda, not explanations. The motives must be other.

What about the alternative view, that it's all about oil? No doubt oil is a crucial element in the operation of the world-economy. And no doubt the United States, like all the other major powers, would like to control the oil situation as much as it can. And no doubt, if Saddam Hussein were overthrown, there would be some reshuffling of the world oil cards. But is the game worth the candle? There are three things about oil that are important: participating in the profits of the oil industry, regulating the world price of oil (which has a great impact on all other kinds of production), and access of supply (as well as potential denial of access to others). In all three matters, the U.S. is doing quite well right now. U.S. oil firms have the lion's share of world profits at the present time. The price of oil has been regulated to U.S. preferences most of the time since 1945, via the efforts of the government of Saudi Arabia. And the U.S. has a fairly good hold on the strategic control of the world oil supply. In each of these three domains, perhaps the U.S. position could be improved. But can this slight improvement possibly be worth the financial, economic, and political costs of war? Precisely because Bush and Cheney have been in the oil business, they must surely be aware of how small would be the advantage. Oil can be at most a collateral benefit of an enterprise undertaken for other motives.

So why, then? We start with the reasoning of the hawks. They are convinced that the world position of the United States has been steadily declining since at least the Vietnam War. They think that the basic explanation for this decline is the fact that U.S. governments have been weak and vacillating in their world policies. (They believe this is true even of the Reagan administration, although they do not dare to say so aloud.) They see a remedy, a simple remedy. The U.S. must assert itself forcefully and demonstrate its iron will and its overwhelming military superiority. Once that is done, the rest of the world will recognize and accept U.S. primacy in everything. The Europeans will fall into line. The potential nuclear powers will abandon their projects. The U.S. dollar will once again rise supreme. The Islamic fundamentalists will fade away or be crushed. And we shall enter into a new era of prosperity and high profit.

We need to understand that they really believe all of this, and with a great sense of certitude and determination. That is why all the public debate, worldwide, about the wisdom of launching a war has been falling on deaf ears. Their ears are deaf because they are absolutely sure that everyone else is wrong and, furthermore, that shortly everyone else will realize they have been wrong. It is important to note one further element in the self-confidence of the hawks. They believe that a swift and relatively easy military victory is at hand—a war of weeks, not of months and certainly not of still longer. The fact that virtually all the prominent retired generals in the U.S. and the U.K. have publicly stated their doubts about this military assessment is simply ignored. The hawks (almost all civilians) do not even bother to answer them. One doesn't know, of course, how many U.S. and U.K. generals still in service are saying, or at least thinking, the same thing.

The full-speed-ahead, torpedoes-be-damned attitude of the Bush administration has already had four major negative effects on the world position of the United States. Anyone with the most elementary knowledge of geopolitics would know that, after 1945, the one coalition the United States had to fear was that of France, Germany, and Russia. U.S. policy has been geared toward rendering this impossible. Every time there was the slightest hint of such a coalition, the U.S. mobilized to break away at least one of the three. This was true when de Gaulle made his early gestures to Moscow in 1945–1946, and when Willy Brandt announced the *Ostpolitik*. There are all sorts of reasons why it has been quite difficult to put together such an alliance. George Bush has overcome the obstacles and achieved the realization of this nightmare for the U.S. For the first time since 1945, these three powers have lined up publicly together against the U.S. on a major issue. U.S. reaction to this public stand is having the effect of cementing the alliance further. If Donald Rumsfeld thinks that waving the support of Albania and Macedonia, or even of Poland and Hungary, in their faces sends shivers up the spines of the new trio, he must be very naive indeed.

The logical riposte to a Paris-Berlin-Moscow axis would be for the U.S. to enter into a geopolitical alliance with China, Korea, and Japan. The U.S. hawks are making sure that such a riposte will not be easily achieved. They have goaded North Korea into displaying its teeth of steel, offended South Korea by not taking its concerns seriously, made China more suspicious than before, and led Japan to think about becoming a nuclear power. Bravo!

Then there's oil. Controlling the world price of oil is the most important of the three oil issues mentioned earlier. Saudi Arabia has been the key. Saudi Arabia has done this work for the U.S. for fifty years for a simple reason. It needed the military protection of the U.S. for the dynasty. The U.S. rush to war, its obvious ricochet effect on the Muslim world, the open disdain of the U.S. hawks for the Saudis, the virtually full support for Sharon have led the Saudis to wonder, out loud, whether U.S. support is not an albatross rather than a mode of sustaining them. For the first time, the faction in the royal house that favors loosening its links with the U.S. seems to be gaining the upper hand. It won't be easy for the U.S. to find a substitute for the Saudis. Remember that the Saudis have always been more important for U.S. geopolitical interests than the Israelis. The U.S. supports Israel for internal political reasons. It has supported the Saudi regime because it has needed them. The U.S. can survive without Israel. Can it survive the political turmoil in the Muslim world without Saudi support?

Finally, U.S. administrations have been valiantly trying to stop nuclear proliferation for fifty years. The Bush administration has managed in two short years to get North Korea and, now, Iran to speed up their programs, and to be unafraid to indicate this publicly. If the U.S. uses nuclear devices in Iraq, as it has hinted it may, it will not merely break the taboo but ensure a speedy race of a dozen more countries to acquire these devices.

If the Iraq war goes splendidly for the U.S., perhaps the U.S. can recuperate a little from these four geopolitical setbacks. If the war goes badly, each negative will be immediately reinforced. I have been reading recently about the Crimean War, in which Great Britain and France went to war against the Russian tyrant in the name of civilization, Christianity, and the struggle for liberty. A British historian wrote about these motives in 1923: "What Englishmen condemn is almost always worthy of condemnation, if only it has happened." The *Times* of London was in 1853 one of the strongest supporters of the war. In 1859, the editors wrote their regret: "Never was so great an effort made for so worthless an object. It is with no small reluctance that we admit a gigantic effort and an infinite sacrifice to have been made in vain." When George Bush leaves office, he will have left the United States significantly weaker than it was when he assumed office. He will have turned a slow decline into a much speedier one. Will the *New York Times* write a similar editorial in 2005?

March 1, 2003: "*The Aftershock*"

If the attack on the Twin Towers on September 11, 2001, can be considered to have been a political earthquake for the American people, the U.S. is now suffering from the aftershock. The most recent and most dramatic instance of that aftershock has come from across the Atlantic and reveals the tectonic shift that transpired largely unnoticed in the last decade.

What was perhaps most unsettling about September 11 was the fact that the U.S., for the first time in its history, felt vulnerable. A direct assault of such magnitude within the continental United States had been previously unknown and unthinkable. The immediate response of people in the rest of the world—most of whom had lived with such vulnerability for a long time—was massively sympathetic. Remember the now-classic editorial title in *Le Monde* of Paris the day after: "We are all Americans now."

In less than eighteen months, the Bush administration has squandered all that sympathy and now finds itself diplomatically isolated. This is the second great shock, the aftershock of September 11. Since 1945, the United States has pursued its global policies with the assurance that it had secure allies—Western Europe, Canada, Japan, and South Korea. To whatever degree one ally or another had reservations about this or that policy, and however much fuss they may have made (a tactic for which France was particularly famous), the United States always counted on the fact that, when the moment of decision came, these allies would be behind the United States.

Up until February 2003, the U.S. government has been sure that the allies' deferral to its leadership in world affairs was a constant on which it could rely. Suddenly this has changed. France and Germany are now leading a "coalition of the unwilling," supported by Russia and China, and overwhelmingly by world public opinion. When the massive peace demonstrations occurred on February 15 across the world, the largest of these took place in the three countries that have most ostentatiously supported the U.S. position on Iraq—Great Britain, Spain, and Italy. In the beginning of March, the U.N. Security Council is going to vote on a U.S.-British-Spanish resolution to legitimate military action against Iraq. They are being met by a French-German-Russian "memorandum" that, in effect, says that there is no justification yet for military action. It is very doubtful that the

U.S. resolution can get the nine votes it needs, even if there is no actual veto.

The immediate result has been a shouting match between the U.S. (with Great Britain), on the one hand, and France and Germany, on the other. It has been much more shrill on the U.S. side than on the Franco-German side. Jacques Chirac, a conservative politician who has spent time in the U.S. and has long been considered one of the French political leaders most friendly toward the U.S., is being vilified and even demonized. How has the relationship of Europe and America deteriorated to the point that the press is asking whether it can ever be repaired, whether we are in the midst of a divorce? To understand that, we have to retrace the story from the beginning—that is, from 1945.

In 1945, the United States was all-powerful, and Western Europe was suffering badly from the economic destruction of the war. Furthermore, a good 25 percent of Western Europe's population was voting for Communist parties, and most of the others genuinely feared that the combination of their internal Communist parties plus the immense Red Army, stationed in the middle of Europe, represented a real threat to their survival as non-Communist states. The alliance of Western Europe with the United States, concretized in the creation of NATO in 1949, had the strong support of a majority of the population, which feared U.S. isolationism more than U.S. imperialism. The U.S. encouraged and supported the establishment of European transnational structures, primarily as a way of making acceptable to the French an involvement of West Germany in the alliance structures.

By the late 1960s, the material and political base of European enthusiasm for the Atlantic alliance began to fritter. Western Europe had revived economically and was no longer dependent on the U.S. Quite the contrary; it was becoming an economic rival! The internal strength of the Communist parties began to dissipate. A Soviet threat began to seem quite distant. Meanwhile, U.S. enthusiasm for European institutions began to wane, as a strong Europe began to seem a risk for the Atlantic alliance. The U.S. encouraged British adhesion, in the hope of diluting Europe (as indeed de Gaulle charged at the time). And later, the U.S. would press for rapid expansion "eastward" in a similar hope.

The collapse of the Soviet Union in 1989–1991 represented a disaster, from the standpoint of U.S. control over its allies. It undid the major justification for U.S. leadership. Who was Western Europe supposed to be afraid of now? The U.S. searched for a substitute for the Soviet Union to offer Western Europe as a reason for faithful adherence to U.S. leadership. Basically, what the U.S. provided was the class interest of the "North" against the "South"—the common interests of the U.S. and Western Europe in global order, neo-liberal globalization, and military containment of the countries of the "South" (that is, continued and intensified insistence on no nuclear proliferation).

These were common interests, indeed, but none of them posed the urgency of the erstwhile Soviet military threat. And Western Europe felt that its approach to particular problems was at least as intelligent and useful as that of Washington. In the days of the first President Bush and of Clinton, these differences led to serious arguments, but the arguments remained civil. Then, along came the hawks of the second President Bush. They were not interested in debating the fine points of what to do in Iraq, Palestine, or North Korea. They felt they knew what to do and they were anxious to make sure that Western Europe accepted, as it had once upon a time, the unquestioned leadership of the U.S. They inherited an old American contempt for the Europe the immigrants had left behind.

However, the geopolitical realities are quite different today. Western Europe feels that Bush's policies in Iraq are as much aimed at them as at Saddam Hussein. They see Bush trying to destroy the possibility of a strong and politically independent Europe, at precisely a very delicate moment in the constitutional construction of this Europe. Furthermore, the defeat of the Socialists in France and the victory of the Social-Democrats in Germany were both serious setbacks for Bush. The Socialists' defeat allowed France, with its curious constitution, to have a president who had the authority to be decisive, because he didn't have to share power with a prime minister of another party. Chirac saw France's interest in asserting its Gaullism unreservedly. In this Chirac has the overwhelming support of French public opinion and politicians, which a Socialist prime minister would never have had. In Germany, on the other hand, only a Social Democratic–Green coalition could have taken the clear stand the government has taken, and found it politically rewarding.

All the bluster of Rumsfeld about how "old Europe" was isolated has been shown to be unfounded. There is not a single country in Europe, including eastern Europe, where the polls are not against the U.S. position. The U.S., which advocates preventive wars and would engage in them unilaterally, is seen as a far greater danger than an encircled and constrained Saddam Hussein. Europe is not anti-American, but it is definitely anti-Bush. Meanwhile, the same thing is happening in East Asia, where Japan, South Korea, and China are aligned against the U.S. approach to handling North Korea.

We shall never go back to the old ways. What will happen now depends a lot on the actual military process of the Iraq war. Europe may emerge much strengthened or in tatters. But the U.S.'s ability to count on automatic support from Western Europe and East Asia is probably gone forever.

April 1, 2003: "*The End of the Beginning*"

At a turning-point in the Second World War, someone asked Winston Churchill whether the battle marked the beginning of the end. And he replied, famously, no, but it might be the end of the beginning. With the Iraq War, the world is marking the end of the beginning of the new world disorder that has replaced the world order dominated by the United States from 1945 to 2001.

In 1945, the United States emerged from the Second World War with so much power in every domain that it quickly established itself as the hegemonic power of the world-system, on which it imposed a series of structures to ensure that it functioned according to the wishes of the United States. The key institutions among them were the United Nations Security Council, the World Bank and IMF, and the Yalta arrangements with the Soviet Union.

What enabled the United States to put these structures in place were three things: (1) the overwhelming edge in economic efficiency of U.S.-based productive enterprises; (2) the network of alliances—especially NATO and the U.S.-Japan Security Treaty—that guaranteed automatic political support of U.S. positions in the U.N. and elsewhere, reinforced by an ideological rhetoric (the "free world") to which the allies of the U.S. were as committed as it was; and (3) a preponderance in the military sphere based on U.S. control of nuclear weapons, combined with the so-called balance of terror with the Soviet Union, which ensured that neither side in the so-called cold war would use these nuclear weapons against the other.

This system worked very well at first. And the U.S. got what it wanted 95 percent of the time, 95 percent of the way. The only hitch was the resistance of those Third World countries not included in the benefits. The most notable cases were China and Vietnam. China's entry into the Korean War necessitated that the U.S. satisfy itself with a truce at the line of departure. And Vietnam in the end defeated the United States—a dramatic shock to the U.S. position politically, and economically as well (since it caused the end of the gold standard and fixed rates of exchange).

An even greater blow to U.S. hegemony was the fact that, after twenty years, both Western Europe and Japan had made such strides economically that they became roughly the economic equals of the United States; thus launched was a long and continuing competition for capital accumulation among these three loci of world production and finance. And then came the world revolution of 1968, which fundamentally undermined the U.S. ideological position (as well as the spuriously oppositional Soviet ideological position).

This triple shock—the Vietnam War, the economic rise of Western Europe and Japan, and the world revolution of 1968—ended the period of easy (and automatic) U.S. hegemony in the world-system. U.S. decline began. The United States reacted to this change in the geopolitical situation with an attempt to slow down its decline as much as possible. We entered a new phase of U.S. world policy—one conducted by all U.S. presidents from Nixon to Clinton (including Reagan). At the heart of this policy were three objectives: (1) maintaining the allegiance of Western Europe and Japan by brandishing the continuing menace of the Soviet Union and offering some say in decision-making (through the so-called partnership represented by the Trilateral Commission and the G-7); (2) keeping the Third World militarily helpless by trying to stanch the "proliferation" of weapons of mass destruction; (3) trying to keep the Soviet Union/Russia and China off-balance by playing one off against the other.

This policy was moderately successful until the collapse of the Soviet Union, which pulled the rug out from under the first key objective. It was this new post-1989 situation that permitted Saddam Hussein to risk invading Kuwait and enabled him to hold the United States to a truce at the line of departure. And it was this geopolitical circumstance, in turn, that permitted the collapse of so many states in the Third World and forced both the United States and Western Europe to engage in basically unwinnable attempts to prevent or eliminate fierce civil wars.

There is one other element to put into this analysis—the structural crisis of the world capitalist system. I have no space here to argue the case, which is made in detail in my book *Utopistics, or Historical Choices of the Twenty-first Century*, but I will resume here with the conclusion. Because the system we have known for 500 years is no longer able to guarantee long-term prospects of capital accumulation, we have entered a period of world chaos. Wild (and largely uncontrollable) swings in the economic, political, and military situations are leading to a systemic bifurcation—that is, to a world collective choice about the kind of new system the world will construct over the next fifty years. The new system will not be a capitalist system, but it could be one of two kinds: a different system that is equally or more hierarchical and inegalitarian, or one that is substantially democratic and egalitarian.

One cannot understand the politics of the U.S. hawks if one does not understand that they are trying not to save capitalism but to replace it with some other, even worse, system. The hawks believe that the U.S.'s world policy pursued from Nixon to Clinton is today unviable and can only lead to catastrophe. They are probably right that it is unviable. What they wish to substitute for it in the short run is a policy of premeditated intervention-ism by the U.S. military, as they are convinced that only the most macho aggressiveness will serve their interests. (I do not say "serve U.S. interests," because I do not believe that it does.)

Osama bin Laden's successful attack on the United States on September 11, 2001, propelled the U.S. hawks into a position where, for the very first time, they con-trolled the short-term policies of the U.S. government. They immediately pushed the necessity of a war on Iraq, seeing it as the first step in implementing their middle-term program. We have arrived at that point. The war has begun. That is why I call this the end of the begin-ning.

Where do we go from here? That depends in part on how the Iraq war plays itself out. One week into the war, it is clearly going less well than the hawks had hoped and anticipated. It seems we are likely to be in for a long, bloody, drawn-out war. The U.S. will proba-bly (but not at all certainly) defeat Saddam Hussein. But its problems will then only mount. If the war goes badly for the U.S. hawks, they will only become more desper-ate. They are likely to try to push harder than ever on their agenda, which seems to have two short-term prior-ities: combat with potential Third World nuclear powers (North Korea, Iran, and others) and establishing an op-pressive police apparatus inside the United States. They will need to win one more election to secure these two objectives. Their economic program seems to be one that will bankrupt the United States. Is this totally unintended? Or do they want to weaken some of the key capitalist strata within the United States, whom they may see as hindering the full implementation of their program?

What is clear at this point is that the world political struggle is sharpening. Those who cling to the U.S. world policy of the 1970–2001 period—the moderate Republicans and the Democratic establishment within the United States, but also in many respects the Western European opponents of the hawks (for example, both the French and the Germans)—may find themselves forced to make more painful political choices than any they have had to make up to now. By and large, this group has lacked middle-range clarity in their analysis of the world situation, and they have been hoping against hope that somehow the U.S. hawks will go away. They will not. The hawks can, however, be defeated.

April 15, 2003: "*Shock and Awe?*"

The U.S. hawks promised us "shock and awe." Have they accomplished it? They think so. But whom were they supposed to shock and awe? Most immediately, the Iraqi regime and its internal supporters. The U.S. did win the war militarily quite rapidly, and those of us (many military figures, but also myself) who had predicted that a long difficult war was the greater possibility were proven wrong. However, the relatively quick victory does, it should be said, undo the argument of the hawks that the Iraqi regime posed a serious military threat to anyone.

Does it follow that those of us who thought the war a folly were wrong on everything else? I don't think so.

In my *Foreign Policy* article (July/August 2002), I opened with the following sentences: "The United States in decline? Few people today would believe the assertion. The only ones who do are the U.S. hawks, who argue vociferously for policies to reverse the decline." The hawks now think they have succeeded in doing this. They are awash with inflated self-confidence. They seem to have adopted Napoleon's motto, "L'audace, l'audace, toujours l'audace." It worked for Napoleon—for a while.

They didn't even wait for the end of the fighting to begin a campaign against Syria—chosen in part because it doesn't have a policy friendly to the U.S., plays a key role in the Middle East, and is militarily virtually helpless. Not having found weapons of mass destruction in Iraq (at least to date), the U.S. government is now suggesting that they are to be found in Syria. Rumsfeld has designated it a "rogue state." President Bush has some simple advice to the Syrians: They should cooperate with the U.S.

Having moved on to Iraq from Afghanistan without achieving anything there other than the overthrow of the previous regime and turning over power to a series of local warlords, will the U.S. now do the same in Iraq, moving on to elsewhere? Quite possibly. And if Syria is next, what comes after Syria? Palestine and Saudi Arabia, or North Korea and Iran? No doubt fierce debates about priorities are going on right now in the inner councils of the U.S. regime. But that the U.S. will now move on to further military threats seems not to be in question. The U.S. hawks seem sure that they have (and ought to have) the world's future in their hands, and they have exhibited not the least sign of humility about the wisdom of their course of action. After all, how many troops does the Pope have, as Stalin famously said?

Still, one should look at the priorities they seem to have established. Number-one seems to be reconfiguring

the Middle East. This includes three key elements: eliminating hostile regimes, undermining the power (and perhaps the territorial integrity) of Saudi Arabia, and
imposing a solution on the Palestinians by getting them
to accept a Bantustan regime. This is why the hawks
have immediately raised the issue of Syria as a new
"threat" to the security of the United States.

While this Middle Eastern reorganization is going
on, the U.S. would, I believe, prefer to freeze the situation in Northeast Asia. Immediate military action is risky,
and the hawks hope to use China to persuade the North
Koreans not to go further in their nuclear quest. One
might think of this as a temporary truce. Such a truce
would allow the U.S. hawks time to deal with other
matters first, North Korea later when their hands would
be freer. For they have no intention of allowing the North
Korean regime to survive.

My guess is that priority number-two is the home
front. The hawks want to shape the U.S. government
budget so that it has no room for anything but military
expenditures. And they will move on all fronts to cut
other expenses—by reducing federal taxes and privatiz-
ing as much of social security and medicare as they can.
They also want to limit the expression of opposition—to
give themselves a freer hand to deal with the rest of the
world, and to ensure their perpetual hold on power. The
immediate issue is making permanent the so-called Patriot Act, which has a clause that causes it to expire in
three years. Thus far, the Patriot Act has been used primarily against persons of Arab or Moslem identity. But
the federal authorities can be expected steadily to expand its reach. On both these fronts, the 2004 elections
are crucial.

Europe is probably priority number-three. It seems
to the hawks harder to break the back of Europe than

that of the Middle East or of the U.S. opposition. So they will probably wait a bit, counting on spreading enough shock and awe so as to weaken fatally the will of the Europeans. In their spare time, the U.S. hawks may ask that troops be sent to Colombia, that the U.S. consider a new invasion of Cuba, and otherwise flex its muscles around the globe.

One must say, the U.S. hawks think big. L'audace, l'audace, toujours l'audace. In that same *Foreign Policy* article, I said: "Today, the United States is a superpower that lacks true power, a world leader nobody follows and few respect, and a nation drifting dangerously amidst a global chaos it cannot control." I reaffirm that assessment today, specifically in the light of the U.S. military conquest of Iraq. My view is based on my belief that U.S. decline in the world-system is structural, not conjunctural. It cannot be reversed. To be sure, it can be managed intelligently, but that is precisely what is not happening now.

The structural decline has two essential components. One is economic, and one is political/cultural. The economic component is really quite simple. In terms of basic capabilities—available capital, human skills, research and development—Western Europe and Japan/East Asia are at a competitive level with the United States. The U.S. monetary advantage—the dollar as a reserve currency—is receding and will probably disappear entirely soon. The U.S. advantage in the military sphere translates into a long-term disadvantage in the economic sphere, since it diverts capital and innovation away from productive enterprises. When the world-economy begins to revive from its now quite long-term stagnation, it is quite likely that both Western European and Japanese/East Asian enterprises will do better than U.S.-based enterprises.

The U.S. has slowed down this creeping economic decline relative to its major competitors for thirty years by political/cultural means, basing its rationale for doing so on residual legitimacy (as the leader of the free world) and the continuing existence of the Soviet Union. The collapse of the Soviet Union undermined this rationale severely and unleashed the growing anarchy of the world-system—"ethnic" wars in the former Soviet zone, civil wars in multiple African states, the two Gulf wars, the expanding cancer of Colombian civil war, and the severe economic recessions in a number of Third World states.

Under Reagan, George Bush the father, and Clinton, the U.S. continued to negotiate with Western Europe and Japan/East Asia to keep them more or less on the same side in what have been essentially North-South struggles. The hawks under George Bush the son have thrown aside this strategy and substituted one of unilateral machismo. The backs of everyone else are up everywhere, and the U.S. victory over Saddam will get them further up, not despite the fact that they are terrified but precisely because of it.

On legitimacy, note two things. In March, the United States had to withdraw a resolution from the U.N. Security Council. This was an issue that was really important to the U.S. and in which it invested all its efforts, including repeated telephone calls by George Bush to leaders around the world. It was the first time in fifty years that the U.S. was unable to get a simple 9-vote majority on the Council. This was humiliation.

Secondly, notice the use of the word *imperial* of late. Until two years ago, speaking of imperialism was the reserve of the world left. But all of a sudden, the hawks started to use the term with a positive connotation. And then, Western Europeans who were not at all on the left began to use the term, worrying that the U.S. was being imperial. And since the collapse of Saddam Hussein, suddenly the word is found in almost every news story. *Imperial(ism)* is a delegitimating term, even if hawks think it is clever to use it.

Military power never has been sufficient, in the history of the world, to maintain supremacy. Legitimacy is essential—at least, legitimacy recognized by a significant part of the world. The U.S. hawks have undermined the claim of the U.S. to legitimacy very fundamentally. And thus they have weakened the U.S. irremediably in the geopolitical arena.

July 1, 2003: *"Common Sense About the Missing Weapons"*

The inability of the United States to find Iraq's famous stock of "weapons of mass destruction" (or WMD, as the newspaper headlines call them) has gotten embarrassing for the Bush regime, and even more so for Tony Blair (as well as the Spanish government). In the rush to justify war, it seems clear that the very least that can be said is that the U.S. and U.K. governments overstated their case, perhaps lied outright.

How important is this? And what does it mean? There are a number of questions intertwined in this discussion. One is How many, if any, weapons did Saddam Hussein really have, and when did he have them? A second is If there were weapons, why didn't he use them? A third is If there were weapons, where are they now? A fourth concerns how important the issue of the weapons really ever was for Bush and Blair? And a fifth is whether or not the world is now safer from whatever menace these weapons were supposed to have posed, now that U.S. troops are in Baghdad. This is a tangled skein of questions, and it is in the interest of many people to keep it tangled, and thus resistant to analytic criticism.

How many weapons did Hussein have? Rumsfeld is now saying that before the war no one (not even the critics of U.S. policy) doubted that he had some, so why all the gloating now about the absence of discoveries? The weapons were there, they are there, and they will be found, says he. He's of course partially right. Very few persons ever doubted the existence of *some* weapons. I myself did not doubt it. The question is whether the weapons represented a significant and imminent threat to the world. The U.S. insisted that they did, and most of the rest of the world disagreed about this assessment rather strongly.

Now it seems Saddam may really have liquidated most, if not all, such weapons as he did have in the months before the war started. No doubt he was under pressure to do so. But then this was just what Hans Blix and the French government had been arguing, when they said that the U.N. inspections were "working." It seems the U.S. has now been able to uncover one Iraqi scientist who admits that detailed documents concerning the construction of nuclear weapons were buried in his garden—over a decade ago. And it seems he says that Saddam ordered this because he was planning to put the plans in operation once sanctions were lifted. That sounds possible to me. But so what? We'll come back to that question.

Did Saddam indeed have operational weapons? Remember, Tony Blair told Parliament that he could put them into the field in 45 minutes. If so, why then didn't he use these weapons? Surely, using them would have had at least some military impact. There is no good answer to this question if we assume the scenarios of which the U.S. had been warning. Maybe, Saddam was cleverer than that. Maybe he figured that he would lose the immediate military battle whatever he did, and the important thing was not to lose all his strongest supporters in the process. In this case, maybe he told them all to melt away, after which they could launch or encourage a looting operation with the double purpose of sowing disorder and destroying infrastructure and records. This might then create a major mess with which the U.S. was politically incapable of dealing (given the complexity of Iraq's social tensions). And then he could start a draining guerrilla war. Too clever, you say? Perhaps. Maybe the U.S. just ended up with the same results without any planning on Saddam's part.

If he had these weapons, where are they now? A batch of plans in a garden and two trucks that might possibly have been used to make biological weapons in the future (and which in any case had been sold to Saddam by the British) are not very much to show for two months of search. I know Iraq is a big country, but presumably the U.S. armed forces are capable of making searches, especially if the U.S. had in its possession before the war started, as it claimed it had, intelligence on where these weapons were. Are these arms in Syria? Unlikely. If they really were, we'd probably have seen the U.S. army go in there by now. Will they turn up in a desert underground site? Perhaps. Why then is the U.S. unwilling to let the U.N. inspectors look for them? It doesn't smell very good.

But was the U.S. ever really interested in whether Iraq had such weapons? The answer is both no and yes. No, in one very important sense. The U.S. hawks wanted to invade Iraq in order to invade Iraq—that is, in order to show the world that the U.S. could and would invade Iraq, just for being a nasty, anti-American focal point in the Middle East. Even if every member of the Bush regime knew for absolute certain that there were not and never had been any weapons of mass destruction, the U.S. would still have invaded Iraq. After all,

Wolfowitz did say that the emphasis on these weapons was just a bureaucratic convenience, meaning it was the kind of argument that might persuade hesitant persons in the U.S. Congress and among the public to support the action, but was never the real reason.

But yes, the U.S. was concerned about weapons of mass destruction, in the sense that the U.S. is determined that no other country or force in the world should be in a position to constrain it in any significant way, and certainly not militarily. This means, as I have said repeatedly, that the U.S. cannot tolerate any form of European Union that would be politically independent of the U.S. And the U.S. cannot tolerate the possession of nuclear weapons by any other country.

Of course, some other countries—the U.K., Russia, France, China, India, Pakistan, and Israel—already do. And the United States knows there is just so much it can do to turn back the clock. But the U.S. policy is to stop any other countries that are conceivably in a position to develop such weapons over the next decade from doing so. This category includes not merely North Korea and Iran, nor even only Libya, Egypt, and Algeria, but also Japan, South Korea, Kazakhstan, Ukraine, Belarus, Germany, South Africa, Brazil, and Argentina. The list is already a long one, but quite possibly dozens of additional countries could be on it.

The reasoning of the U.S. is really quite simple. The damage that can be done by even one small atomic bomb dropped in the course of warfare is sufficient to make the price of U.S. military action very high, perhaps too high. There is much talk these days of asymmetrical warfare, meaning that the U.S. is so far ahead of any other country in terms of military weaponry that it necessarily must win any encounter. But the so-called WMD can undo that asymmetry, especially given the political impact that the use of such weapons by others against the U.S. would have on U.S. public opinion and the willingness to sanction warfare.

So, it is understandable that the U.S. would try so hard to stem proliferation. Nonetheless, one has to say that this attempt is a quixotic quest if ever there was one. For one thing, changing governments (regime change) does not solve the problem in the least. We need to remember today that Iran's nuclear program was started not by the ayatollahs but by the shah, whom the U.S. put into power, and that it was abetted by the Israelis, who saw Iran as a constraint on Iraq. We also have to remember that Iraq's biological warfare program was aided and abetted by the British and the Americans when they saw Iraq as a constraint on Iran. And so on.

Far from slowing down the programs to create WMD capacity everywhere, the U.S. invasion of Iraq has speeded them up. Meanwhile, the U.S. is caught up in a long, draining occupation of Iraq, with lessened, not increased, ability to protect its interests across the world. On June 30, the *Financial Times* queried whether Iraq had become Bush's Chechnya. And Bush's cynical use of the WMD issue vis-à-vis Hussein will catch up with him, as U.S. soldiers come under increasing fire in the guerrilla war that has started.

George W. Bush will learn the lesson of every ruler. There are limits to power, especially if it is not used prudently and intelligently. Seldom, in recent history, has it been used so extravagantly and so recklessly.

July 15, 2003: *"When Will Bush Fall?"*

Bush's days are numbered. He is in serious trouble, and the trouble will not go away. The tissue of justifications for the Iraq invasion is fraying bit by bit. Both he and Blair have had to retreat from some of the more egregious statements. The famous weapons of mass destruction are nowhere to be found. And if some turn out to be deeply buried somewhere, all that will prove is that the weapons were not readily usable in a war—certainly not in the famous 45-minute interval cited by Tony Blair. The aluminum tubes seem to be exactly what Saddam Hussein said they were, material for rockets. The asserted ties between Saddam Hussein and al-Qaeda were always improbable, and no evidence has been adduced to confirm them. Bush has now laid the blame on the CIA, while the Republican chair of the Senate Intelligence Committee is accusing the CIA of leaking material to embarrass President Bush. The thieves are falling out.

The U.S. lived through this scenario once before, and not too long ago. The Watergate cover-up of President Nixon worked at first, with only partisan sniping for a long while. But when Nixon tried to point the finger at fall guys (remember John Dean), they started to reveal the truth. Nixon did win his reelection. He held out that long. But in the end, he had to resign the presidency when a successful impeachment was imminent.

Of course, the two situations are quite different in their details. But there are certain striking similarities. They both took place within the context of the ambivalence of U.S. public opinion about a war. They both involved presidents who were willing to use all the instruments at their command to ram through policies and intimidate opponents. They both had persons around them who were masters at stonewalling. Vice-President Cheney must have taken lessons at the feet of Nixon's attorney-general, John Mitchell.

In politics—world politics, national politics, local politics—you can get a lot of support if you're winning. But the support often flees as soon as you start to lose. Bush promised the U.S. and the world a transformation of Iraq—indeed, of the Middle East—if only Saddam Hussein could be ousted. At this point, about three months after the military collapse of the Iraqi regime, what is the situation in Iraq? Every day, American soldiers are being killed by what is clearly a guerrilla action of some consequence. Iraqi policemen, newly appointed by the U.S. occupiers, threatened to resign if U.S. soldiers did not quit their police station, believing that their lives were in danger for too close an association with the U.S. army. Apparently, U.S. soldiers are seen not as protectors of those who cooperate with them but as a force that endangers lives.

The U.S. occupiers have been unable to restore even a minimum of electricity in the urban centers of Iraq. Frankly, I am amazed by this. One would think that the U.S. government could assemble the necessary engineers, fly in the necessary equipment, and supply the necessary protection to the engineers so that electricity could be restored in a week or two. Is it too expensive? Are there other priorities? Does the U.S. not think this is important? Ordinary Iraqis think it's the number-one priority and are getting very angry. Soon, the country may be awash with nostalgia for the regime the U.S. ousted.

Meanwhile, in Great Britain, the heroic ally of the U.S., Tony Blair is in increasingly deep trouble. The Conservatives have decided there is no profit in supporting him. The Liberals never did. And the number of Labour M.P.s who are restive is growing. At just this moment, the U.S. has announced that at Guantánamo Bay it is going to try six persons, of whom two are British citizens. There is a storm brewing in Great Britain among very respectable jurists who object to what they see as dubious, even illegal, procedures. They are calling for

Blair to get the U.S. to turn these men over to British justice. But Blair can't promise the U.S. that confessions extracted in the absence of legal counsel will stand up in British courts. There is no easy way that the U.S. could help Blair in this difficulty without jeopardizing the entire structure of the Guantánamo nightmare. At the same time, the U.S. government is having a very hard time convincing any U.S. attorneys to be defense attorneys because they assert that the rules are rigged against them illegitimately.

The U.S. victory in Iraq was supposed to have the effect of getting recalcitrant allies—France, Germany, Russia—to reverse their positions. There is no sign of this whatsoever. Why should they? When *Time* magazine conducted a poll in Europe in March, asking which of three countries—North Korea, Iraq, or the United States—was the biggest threat to world peace, a whopping 86.9 percent answered the United States. And the U.S. and Europe are on a collision course about mundane trade matters. In this, the U.S. clearly has the weaker position. The World Trade Organization is ruling against the U.S. on these matters. Lots of little countries are quietly, and some not so quietly, refusing to bend to the U.S. insistence on being the only country above international law.

And last but not least, the U.S. economy is not doing well at all. In addition, there are conservatives yelling that the Bush regime is not really conservative, because it is increasing, not reducing, the role of the state. Howard Dean is taking off as a potential Democratic candidate. And even if he doesn't get the nomination, which he in fact may, he has already forced the other Democratic candidates to "move to the left" to try to capture a little of the support Dean seems to be getting.

Can Bush turn all this around? In the short run, maybe. If he can capture Saddam Hussein, that would help

Bush. Here again, I am amazed that the U.S. has not been able to do this. But perhaps I should not be so amazed. Osama bin Laden has not been captured, dead or alive, in the almost two years Bush has been chasing him. Mullah Omar is still at large, and it seems he has been reorganizing the Taliban.

As for the hawks who surround Bush, the day after the fall of Baghdad they started clamoring to invade Syria. But all that's quiet now. Neither Iran nor North Korea has slowed down its drive to acquire nuclear weapons. Quite the contrary. Both are virtually flaunting it. And the U.S. is being very prudent. The U.S. does not seem to have even the troops available to do what is urgently needed, reinforcing their position in Iraq. It seems scarcely in a position to take Iran or North Korea seriously. Nor are the diplomatic initiatives achieving much of anything—in Israel/Palestine, in Northeast Asia, or even in Latin America.

If I were George W. Bush, I'd be very worried. Perhaps he's not. Pride goeth before the fall. But I bet some of his clever political advisors are chewing their nails. They were feeling very sure of themselves not so long ago. But the ship of state has hit rough water. It may not sink immediately. But will it reach shore safely? The odds are not high enough for them to be smiling complacently.

August 1, 2003: *"Has Saddam Hussein Lost?"*

The answer, say the American authorities, is obvious. Paul Bremer, the U.S. proconsul in Iraq, said recently, "Dead or alive, this man is finished in Iraq." What is wrong with this analysis is that it is made from the narrow viewpoint of someone who plays the game of geopolitics from a position of habitual strength, and who therefore measures wins and losses in a very short-term perspective. But the game of geopolitics looks different if you play it from a position of relative weakness. In that case, you have to play for the middle run. Let us look at how the war in Iraq might look from the position of Saddam Hussein.

In 1958, radical nationalists overthrew the monarchy in Iraq and installed Abdul Karim Kassim in power. The government considered itself pan-Arabist and revolutionary. Kassim took Iraq out of the U.S.-backed Baghdad Pact. He nationalized part of the oil industry. He had the support of the Communist Party of Iraq. He seemed to the U.S. to be moving to align Iraq too closely with the Soviet Union. In 1963, there was a second coup, which installed the Baath Party in power. The Baath Party had been a secular, socialist, nationalist pan-Arab movement in several Arab countries but was hostile to the Communist parties. It is widely believed the CIA helped the Baath to come to power. The Baath Party suppressed the Communist Party of Iraq.

At the time, Saddam Hussein was a young, up-and-coming Baath leader, nephew of the new president, intelligent and ruthless. In 1979, he staged a bloody coup against his uncle and became the ruler of Iraq. He began his unceasing purge of opponents. What did Saddam want, besides merely being in power? He wanted to strengthen the Arab role in world politics. He was in favor of greater Arab unity, and probably saw himself as the natural leader of the Arab world, the new Saladin. No doubt there were other aspirants for this role, but with Nasser out of the picture, none was as strong. Besides, Baghdad had always been, along with Cairo, the claimant to central status in the Arab-Muslim world.

Saddam saw his objectives as having many enemies. In the Arab world, the two main ones were the Communists and the Islamists, and both hated Saddam. In the rest of the world, the two main ones were Iran and Israel, which hated Saddam, and the United States and Russia, both of which hoped Saddam hated the other more. Saddam couldn't fight all his enemies at once. Without cutting ties with the Soviet Union, he struck up a tacit accord with the United States in the days of Ronald Reagan. None other than Donald Rumsfeld came to Iraq to seal the deal. What was the deal? Iraq attacked Iran. This was partly to gain territory, partly to weaken the Shia opponents inside Iraq, partly to achieve pan-Arab prestige, partly to strengthen Saddam's own military. The United States, at the time regarding Iran as the chief danger to its interests in the Middle East, thought this was a wonderful idea and gave—both directly and via its allies such as Saudi Arabia—armaments, biological and chemical weapons, and intelligence support to Saddam Hussein. (To be fair, it had been the French at an earlier time who had given the Iraqis their first boost in the drive to obtain nuclear weapons, but then the Israelis bombed these facilities.)

The Iraq-Iran war was a bust from Saddam's perspective. After eight years of struggle, both countries were back at the starting-point, having suffered massive loss of lives and resources. Still, the war kept the Iranians busy and this was a plus for the United States. Saddam demanded recompense. Both the U.S. and Saudi Arabia were slow in responding. At just this moment, the Soviet Union collapsed. The cold war was over. Saddam Hussein saw this as a bonanza, not a negative. The Soviet Union had been a continuing arms supplier for Iraq. But the price for that was that Iraq could not do anything to strain U.S.-Soviet relations. Saddam was now free from this constraint, at last.

In 1990, Iraq was in economic trouble, with the price of oil low on the world market and the costs of the Iraq-

Iran war having been heavy. Kuwait was insisting on being repaid for its loans during the war. It may also have been stealing Iraqi oil via diagonal drilling. And Iraq had a historic claim to Kuwait, which it charged had been part of its zone in the Ottoman era and was arbitrarily separated from Iraq by the British after the First World War. So, Saddam decided that the solution to his economic problems was to seize Kuwait. Doing so also fulfilled an Iraqi nationalist claim and, if successful, would make Iraq the number-one Arab nation. Iraq could even be the savior of Palestine, the negotiations between the PLO and the Israelis having just broken down.

Saddam's calculations were probably as follows. Invading Kuwait will no doubt be called aggression. But can I get away with it? Who will respond? Only the United States would be in a position to do anything serious, and the U.S. had long been ambivalent in its relations with Iraq. As we now know, the U.S. ambassador, April Glaspie, told Saddam just days before the invasion that the U.S. was neutral in the Iraq-Kuwait diplomatic argument. So, Saddam reasoned, either the U.S. will react or it will fudge.

If it fudged, Saddam would have won. If it reacted, there would be a war. At most, Iraq would probably come out a nonloser, for the U.S. would not dare to invade Iraq. He was of course correct, for the reasons that President George H. W. Bush and General Schwarzkopf gave at the time. An invasion would have been too costly in U.S. lives, the occupation would have been too costly politically, and Saudi Arabia and Turkey feared a breakup of Iraq as well as the consequent creation of a Shia state in the south and a Kurdish state in the north.

So, when the first Gulf War ended, Saddam managed a truce at the line of departure. He did suffer some losses. Parts of his army and air force had been lost. A de facto Kurdish state was established in the north, but not a Shia state in the south. He was subjected to a U.N. regime to end his weapons of mass destruction. By the time he was able to evict the U.N. inspectors in 1998, most of his weapons of mass destruction were no more.

When George W. Bush came to power, Saddam knew he was in trouble, as most of Bush's chief advisors had publicly called for overthrowing Saddam just a few years before. Then came 9/11. And Saddam must have known that it would be he, not Osama bin Laden, who would pay the price. So he called back the U.N. inspectors, knowing they would find nothing, since by now it seems he had destroyed or not replaced the destroyed weapons of mass destruction. It soon became clear, however, that nothing Saddam did would stop the U.S. invasion, since the point of the invasion was to remove Saddam and establish U.S. might in the region.

Why, then, if he no longer had weapons of mass destruction, did he not say so? Well, as a matter of fact, he did, but no one believed him. So, what could he do? He knew the limited power of his own army, and he knew that he would lose the second Gulf War. If you were Saddam and knew you would lose the second Gulf War, what would you do? Obviously, prepare for the third Gulf War. How could you do that? The first thing you'd do would be to make sure that as many of your relatively small contingent of fierce loyalist fighters would survive. Therefore, you would have the resistance collapse early and dramatically. The second thing you would do is to create massive disorder by systematic looting. The third thing you would do is start a guerrilla war, aimed first of all at U.S. soldiers and second of all at collaborators.

Then you'd sit back and wait for the erosion of the U.S. position. You would expect that two crucial public opinions would shift in time. In the United States, the creeping losses of lives, the inability to get things going in Iraq, and the patent deceptions of the Bush regime would erode U.S. support for the operation. And in Iraq, as time went on, the image of Saddam the torturer would give way to the image of Saddam the nationalist resister. Even if the U.S. were to find and kill Saddam, his image might survive. And in any case, the image of the U.S. as the liberator would disintegrate.

This is less good than being Saladin, but if you're weak, you have to settle for what you can get. Bush thinks that if he brings down Saddam, he will have won. But Saddam thinks that if he brings down Bush, he will have won. We shall see who is right.

October 15, 2003: "*Osama's Victory*"

The attacks of 9/11 on the Twin Towers and the Pentagon have been attributed to Osama bin Laden and al-Qaeda, and have been called acts of terrorism. What is the meaning of terrorism? What is its purpose? *Terrorism* is usually defined as acts perpetrated against a category of victims with the objective of sowing terror—that is, excessive fear on the part of others in the victims' category. It is done in an attempt to make these others change their future behavior. In this case, the victims were generically American civilians. (I know there were others in the buildings, but that was in some sense, from the viewpoint of the terrorists, accidental.) The first question, then, is Did the attacks succeed in sowing terror among Americans, thereby changing their future behavior?

If one read the *New York Times* of September 12, 2003, which no doubt neither Osama bin Laden nor George

W. Bush did, one might be tempted to say that yes, indeed, the attacks succeeded because they changed the behavior of the kinds of people who were attacked, in ways that, for Osama bin Laden, were a victory. The United States used to boast of being an open society, where people could come and go as they pleased, a country welcoming of visitors and immigrants, a country in which the police were not oppressive, a country in which ordinary people were not afraid.

What do we find in the newspaper stories? There is one Reuters story entitled "Security around U.S. Embassy strains relations with Berlin," which begins: "The tight security that has sealed the American Embassy here from the rest of Berlin and brought a once bustling block in the heart of the German capital to a standstill has an eerie cold war feel to it. Fences 10 feet high, huge concrete barriers, guards with machine guns and armored vehicles have made the street in front of the five-story building look like a war zone, disrupting businesses and motorists." The story discusses the great unhappiness of Berliners, the disputes with the city government about the extent of the cordon around the embassy, and the fact that neither the British nor the French embassies have felt the need to install similar security measures. It ends by quoting a Dutch tourist: "I don't know if there needs to be so much security here. It seems like way too much. It makes you feel like you aren't free."

The second story, entitled "In-transit foreign fliers deterred by new rules," details the consequences of the fact that the U.S. government now requires many persons from other countries who merely change planes in a U.S. airport to obtain visas in advance, even if these persons do not go beyond the transit lounge. Who are such people? Well, Brazilians flying to Japan passing through New York, or Costa Ricans flying to Spain passing through Miami. It also talks about tourists from central Europe coming on visits to the United States—the excessive costs and time of acquiring the tourist visa in Slovakia, the fact that Czechs are in a dilemma when answering U.S. consuls' queries about military service because it seems Czech law makes it a crime to disclose military service. One result is that a Czech tourist agency has decided to send people to Canada instead: Not only is there no visa hassle, but the Canadian government actually offers to help with trip planning.

The third story is entitled "Aid workers leaving Iraq, fearing they are targets." At the very moment that the U.S. government is asking the world to assist it in the reconstruction of Iraq, "the great majority of foreign aid workers in Iraq, fearing they have become targets of the new violence, have quietly pulled out of the country in the past month, leaving essential relief work to their Iraqi colleagues and slowing the reconstruction effort." This is because the aid workers either are Americans, are mistaken for Americans, or are associated in Iraqi minds with the U.S. occupying authority. So, even if they are French, they have to fear being mistaken for Americans.

None of the three stories relates an issue of world-shaking importance. But together, two years after the attacks of September 11, they indicate that—from the U.S.'s point of view—the situation is far from being in hand. The U.S. has had to retreat behind walls of safety—in Berlin, concrete barriers around its embassy, creating obstacles to foreign tourism; and in Baghdad, both the loss of civilian aid workers and the placement of its own people behind other concrete barriers. No doubt some, perhaps even all, of these security measures are justified by the dangers posed. But that's the point. That's just what Osama bin Laden hoped and expected would happen.

It is a victory for him because living behind concrete barriers is, first of all, a severe limitation on the freedoms of those who have to do this. And secondly, living behind walls breeds an ambiance of fear and besiegement, which inevitably affects behavior at home and abroad. I suppose if one presents this analysis to officials of the Bush administration, they will answer that the "war on terror" is supposed to end this state of fear and besiegement, by eliminating the source of the fear. One has the right to wonder, after reading the newspaper accounts, whether this "war on terrorism" has been effective, whether the Bush administration has in fact done what was actually necessary to eliminate the source of the fear. The fact is that, at the present time, the fear is growing, not diminishing. It behooves us to ask why.

November 15, 2003: "*What Is Realism in Iraq?*"

As the U.S. gets into more and more difficulty in Iraq, the U.S. hawks are becoming increasingly shrill in their attacks on the doubters. They are accusing the doubters of being out of touch with what is going on. And this, they say, is what is causing the U.S. difficulty. So in the end it is not the Iraqis but the messengers of skepticism who are said to be causing the harm to U.S. interests. I myself was attacked for being an example of "dizzying unreality" in an article by Victor Davis Hanson in the October 13, 2003, issue of the *National Review*, America's premier conservative journal of opinion. Here is the evidence Hanson offers:

> Immanuel Wallerstein warned of the possibility of "a long and exhausting war," dismissing the scenario of a quick triumph—"Swift and easy victory, obviously the hope of the U.S. administration, is the least likely [outcome]. I give

> it one chance in twenty"—before concluding that "losing,
> incredible as it seems (but then it seemed so in Vietnam
> too), is a plausible outcome."

Hanson's quotes, taken from an article I wrote in *Foreign Policy* in its July/August 2002 issue, don't seem to me, today, anything I should blush about. It is true that I, along with most people, expected Saddam Hussein to hunker down in the big cities and fight a house-by-house war. But, it seems, he was cleverer than we were. He decided instead on a guerrilla war. Scott Ritter, an American ex-marine who was part of the U.N. inspection teams of the mid-1990s, says he came across, at that time, an outline of an official program for a guerrilla war in case of invasion, a document that he turned over to U.S. authorities. And in the November 13, 2003, issue of the *Washington Post*, the commanding general of the 82nd Airborne Division, Major General Charles H. Swannack, Jr., who is responsible for combat operations in the lower Sunni triangle, is quoted as being in essential agreement with this assessment: "I believe Saddam Hussein always intended to fight an insurgency should Iraq fall. That's why you see so many of these arms caches out there in significant numbers all over the country. They were planning to go ahead and fight an insurgency."

So, let us review where we are. The U.S. clearly has not won a swift and easy victory. The U.S. is in a long, drawn-out war. In that article I wrote last year, I said I thought the U.S. had two chances out of three of winning a long, drawn-out, bloody war and only one in three of a real defeat. But a recent widely leaked supposedly top-secret CIA report says that the U.S. might actually be losing the situation in Iraq. I may thus have overestimated the chances of the U.S. to win. In any case, it would be a dizzying unreality to believe that the U.S. is doing well in the Iraq fiasco.

We now know, because no less than Richard Perle, the preeminent neo-con, tells us, that Saddam Hussein offered just before the U.S. invasion, via a backdoor messenger, to make a deal that would have left him in power but allowed direct U.S. inspection for weapons of mass destruction. The offer was not pursued by the U.S. The commentary on this revelation by the *New York Times* in its editorial of November 7, 2003, was as follows:

> Administration supporters were fond of saying at the time that there were things Bush officials knew but could not share with the public. Little did we imagine that among those things was an offer that might have provided a way to avoid the war.

Meanwhile, within the United States, all the polls show that the U.S. public is slowly but surely coming to the conclusion that the whole Iraq adventure was a mistake. One of the most senior U.S. senators, Ernest "Fritz" Hollings, a Democrat from South Carolina, with thirty years of service, made a not widely reported speech on November 3 on the floor of the Senate explaining his misgivings about Iraq. Hollings started by saying, "I come to acknowledge my 'Cambodian moment' in the Iraq war." He was referring to an earlier war, when Senator Mansfield of Montana, the then–Majority Leader in the U.S. Senate, said at the time of the invasion of Cambodia that he could not take the Vietnam War any longer. Hollings said he did not want to wait as long as Mansfield did on Vietnam.

What is important about this speech is that Hollings is from the South and has been historically a quite conservative Democrat. And countering the Bush regime's hype, he asserts that to say this isn't Vietnam all over again is nonsense. The rumbling in middle America that Hollings represents is very real and is spreading very fast.

So could the United States really lose the war in Iraq? Well, the U.S. really did lose the war in Vietnam. Of course, I suppose it depends on how you would define winning the war. Do we mean a situation in which U.S. troops remain in Iraq but no one shoots at them? The real prospect before us is, instead, the gathering of U.S. troops in Iraq behind concrete walls where it's more difficult to shoot at them. Does it mean the election of a "democratic" government? A free election today, or tomorrow, would most likely lead to a Shiite majority, and not to a government in the hands of those favored exiles the U.S. has been sponsoring. In either case, it is doubtful that those elected would consider John Locke or Thomas Jefferson their heroes, or have a less hostile view toward Israel than Saddam Hussein, or be less likely to pursue nuclear proliferation as soon as they could. After all, Iraq has national interests too, and these don't accord very well with the national interests of the United States.

The U.S. administrator in Iraq, Paul Bremer, seemed to think he could handle this dilemma by remaining proconsul in Iraq for a long time and slowly building an acceptable puppet regime. But the daily deaths make even the hawks in Washington doubt that they have the leisure to be so disingenuous. The horizon is grim for the United States in Iraq, in the Middle East, and indeed in the world.

This puts the Bush administration in a bind. In Washington, they are now beginning to mumble about an exit strategy. Some think this may win more votes for Bush in 2004 than persisting in the current strategy. But it may also lose votes among disillusioned partisans. So it's a lose-lose situation for Bush. And the only dizzying unreality would be not to recognize this.

January 1, 2004: "*2003—The Year of Bush*"

The year 2003 is the year in which George W. Bush left his mark on the world. As the new year began, he was probably celebrating the previous one. But in actuality it was a disastrous year—for Bush, for the United States, and for the world. What Bush sought to demonstrate was that the United States could and would assert its power unilaterally in the world, succeed militarily in doing so, and thereby strengthen its political and economic position in the world. The U.S. would show it was the superpower—if not one that was respected, then at least one that was feared, by friend and foe alike. Has he succeeded? I think not.

Let us look at the year's events from Bush's point of view. The year started out rather badly. In February, the U.S. sought international legitimization for its war on Iraq via a resolution of the U.N. Security Council. Despite heavy lobbying, including repeated telephone calls by the president himself, the U.S. was unable to secure more than 4 votes (out of 15) for such a resolution and hence withdrew it. In March, the U.S. invaded Iraq anyway, with a "coalition of the willing"—essentially Great Britain, Australia, and Poland. At the last minute, Turkey, despite the large monetary bribe that it was offered, refused to take part.

The military operation was nonetheless swift, and by May the U.S. had occupied more or less all of Iraq. Bush proclaimed that the mission had been "accomplished." But as soon as he said that, the guerrilla war began, and it has been growing in strength ever since. More U.S. troops have been killed and many more wounded since the mission was "accomplished" than in the first phase, and as the year ended the U.S. armed

forces admitted that the rate of casualties was mount-
ing, not diminishing. Although the U.S. has worked hard
to get other countries to send troops, its success has
been quite limited. As a result, the U.S. has not yet been
able to reduce its own troop commitment.

December brought one bright quasi-military achieve-
ment, the capture of Saddam Hussein. The head of the
U.S. occupation, Paul Bremer, announced: "Ladies and
gentlemen, we got him." And so they had. But since this
was not a child's game of hide-and-seek, it is not clear
that the capture of Saddam solved many problems for
the U.S. It was no doubt psychologically encouraging,
especially inside the U.S. But did it reduce resistance to
the U.S. occupation? It may possibly have been dis-
couraging to some Baathist loyalists, although this remains
to be proved. But, on the other hand, it liberated those
Iraqis who had previously hesitated to fight against the
U.S. only because they feared Saddam's return. Iraqi nationalism, after all, is not dependent on Saddam Hussein.
In any case, the last weeks of December showed a considerable increase in violent attacks on the occupying forces.

How did Bush fare on the world economic and political fronts? Economically, the war brought about the so-
called Baghdad boost, allowing for a spurt of growth
worldwide. This was in large part the result of U.S. military Keynesianism. But there are two downsides to be
noticed. The economic growth has largely benefited the
wealthy. It did not result in a reduction in unemployment, either in the United States or elsewhere, or in an
increase in real income for the working strata. So the
longer-term impact on effective demand is in doubt. And,
even more important, the dollar has been careening
downward.

The downward slide of the dollar is, to be sure, an
economic plus for Bush in the very short run (that is, in

the electoral year of 2004). It permits an increase in U.S. exports and a reduction in real terms of the external debt. It may have stanched a further rise in unemployment. But a strong dollar is in the end a powerful political and economic tool, and the U.S. cannot afford to have a weak dollar for very long. But can it do anything to reverse the downslide? To cover the external accounts deficit, the U.S. borrows money by selling its bonds each month. Until 2003, it was able to sell enough to cover its increasing deficit and, hence, make possible the incredible financial transfers to U.S. corporations and its wealthiest citizens.

But, as the dollar began to lose significant value, the rest of the world stopped throwing good money after bad by continuing to buy bonds whose value was plummeting. The U.S. deficit is no longer being covered by dollar inflow, which poses dilemmas for the U.S. Treasury. And total immediate disaster is averted only by the decision of East Asian governments, particularly China, to continue buying U.S. Treasury notes. China as well as Japan and South Korea do this out of self-interest, of course. But their investment in dollars puts them at risk as well, and they may soon decide that the advantages are outweighed by the dangers to their own resources. In any case, the United States is now dependent on them for its continuing economic health, not vice versa, which is hardly a position of economic strength. And meanwhile, the U.S. is up for sale to outside investors, the inverse of what the U.S. would like the situation to be.

Politically, the situation is not much better. The war in Iraq marked a turning-point in U.S. political relations with Europe. France, Germany, and Russia have shifted from being recalcitrant allies to being uncomfortable but systematic political rivals. They act warily with the

United States, not collusively. As a result, while they may from time to time go along with something the U.S. proposes, the U.S. can no longer count on them in a pinch. The repayment of the Iraqi debt is a case in point. James Baker seems to have obtained commitments from the European and East Asian debtors to renounce some part of the Iraqi debt. These countries may have despaired of being paid in any case, and they may yet exact concessions about rights to future arrangements with Iraq as the price of debt cancellation, when the detailed negotiations take place. Baker has not yet gotten the Arab states, which are the biggest creditors, to do the same. It should not be forgotten that one of the motives of the Iraqi invasion of Kuwait was to annul the debt owed to Kuwait.

It is now being openly said that Western Europe is not ready to become, once again, a faithful follower of American leadership. Most political figures, even the more conservative ones, believe that U.S. policy in the Middle East is fundamentally flawed—with respect not only to Iraq but also to Afghanistan, Iran, and Israel/ Palestine. If either Pakistan or Saudi Arabia blows up in the face of the United States, there will be *Schadenfreude* in most European capitals, even in eastern Europe.

Last but certainly not least, the electoral campaign promises to be very difficult for George Bush. At the moment, he is counting primarily on the curtailment of the deflation threat and the capture of Saddam Hussein to propel his campaign forward. But Bush has raised hackles not only in the rest of the world. He has aroused a sleepy U.S. electorate to passionate political involvement. He has his devoted following, but for a significant portion of the American population, he arouses the strongest possible opposition. There will undoubtedly be some swing voters attracted by his patriotic rhetoric. But there are also large numbers (probably larger numbers) of nonvoting youths, greens, Blacks, and Latinos who have become deeply fearful of a Bush second term and are ready to vote this time.

The year 2004 may not be the year of Bush.

February 15, 2004: *"The War President Sinking in the Mire"*

"I'm a war president," George W. Bush told Tim Russert on NBC's *Meet the Press* on February 8, 2004. The statement only makes his case weaker. President Bush has had his former secretary of the treasury, Paul O'Neill, testify that war against Iraq was on the cabinet's agenda from the day Bush took office. So, it wasn't September 11 that led Bush on this path. And having told the American people and the world, not once but again and again, that Saddam Hussein's weapons of mass destruction posed an urgent threat to the United States and the world, Bush heard his hand-picked head of the Iraq Survey Group, David Kay, who was charged with finding Saddam's weapons, testify to the U.S. Congress that he couldn't find any and that he now believed Saddam Hussein gave them up as early as 1991.

Bush's standing in the polls fell immediately, and even quite conservative commentators are upset by Kay's findings and by the fact that the U.S. went to war on false pretenses. Everyone now wants to know how U.S. intelligence went awry, as if that were the problem. It is clear that the intelligence, which was itself faulty, has been vastly overinterpreted by the Bush administration to meet its preconceived objectives. And it is not true that "everyone was wrong." After all, before the war there were clear voices—those of the head of the International Atomic Energy Agency, Scott Ritter, and others—pointing out the lack of evidence that weapons existed.

Bush is on the defensive. Different stories are arising out of the coterie that surrounds him. Colin Powell, like Bush himself, now is not sure there were such weapons. Cheney and Rumsfeld are still saying they expect them to turn up. But no matter. The justification has changed. Bush tells us that Saddam Hussein had "the capacity to produce weapons." And besides, "he was a dangerous man," and "this is a dangerous world." Saddam Hussein is/was a "madman" who could potentially make a weapon and "then let that weapon fall into the hands of a shadowy terrorist network." In addition, "when the United States says there will be serious consequences, and if there aren't serious consequences, it creates adverse consequences." Eventually (who knows?), he might have made a nuclear weapon and then the U.S. "would have been in a position of blackmail."

It's gotten to be so thin an explanation that the United States today has lost all credibility, probably even with Tony Blair, who alas would never admit it. Meanwhile, things in Iraq are not going well at all. Five to ten Americans are being killed each week. And it's mighty dangerous to try to enroll in the Iraqi police force. Iraqi women are now afraid to leave their homes because of fundamentalist pressures. Iraq's code governing women, formerly the most progressive in the Arab world, has just been repealed by the Iraqi interim authority in favor of the sharia. The United States would dearly like to get out as soon as possible from the quagmire in which it said it would never be caught. It would like to turn over sovereignty to an Iraqi government by June 30. It would like the United Nations to take over post-June supervision of political negotiations among the Iraqis. It would like NATO to take over managing a stabilization

force. It is not clear that it can achieve any of these wishes.

The June 30 turnover to Iraqis is bogged down at the
moment because the Shia are insisting on elections (democracy, remember?), which they would win. The Kurds
are insisting on virtual self-rule. And the Sunnis are insisting on not losing everything. The Shia and the Kurds
have military units in existence, and the Sunnis are no
doubt going to create one. The United States has suddenly produced a document showing that all this ethnic
conflict is an al-Qaeda plot. The reality is that it will be
miraculous if post-June there isn't a rather unpleasant
civil war. If the United States thinks that Kofi Annan
and NATO want to get caught up in the middle of that,
it better think again. The *Neue Zürcher Zeitung*, Switzer-
land's leading newspaper and scarcely a newspaper
hostile to the U.S., has just run a cartoon showing a
cement mixer labeled "Iraq reconstruction" pouring over
George Bush in military costume and already half-bur-
ied in the cement. Looking on are bemused spectators
labeled "U.N." and "Europe," to whom Bush says somewhat desperately, "Well, if you really insist on giving a
hand."

The problem is that George Bush has nowhere to go.
He has a difficult election coming up, and lots to explain
about his own Vietnam war record. He can bluster all he
wants about how nuclear proliferation is such a great
danger that everyone should give up making even nuclear fuel for peaceful purposes, or face the consequences. Meanwhile, he is proposing to expand the nuclear
bomb capacity of the United States. So, we may expect a
rush of countries to cease nuclear fuel production.

And then there's the little matter of the economic hole
he's been digging for the United States. If you give back
most of the taxes and mightily expand war expenditures,

of course the deficit is going to rise to astronomical proportions. He is scaring the pants off the serious capitalists of the world. Even some of the ultra-right-wing economic conservatives in Congress are threatening to abstain in the next elections because of the endlessly rising deficit.

Bush did leave us with one last consolation in that interview with Tim Russert on NBC. He said, "A free Iraq will change the world." I'm hoping myself that a free Iraq, if ever we and the Iraqis get there, might even change the United States. Who knows? It will be Bush's legacy.

Part III

The Possible and the Desirable

Those who criticize Bush for his "unilateralism" seem to think that all the U.S. needs to do to put the country back on track is to return to the strategies of the past thirty years, and the glass would become at least half full again. This is an illusion. As noted earlier, the reason I call the previous strategies "*soft* multilateralism" is that the U.S. never really meant it. Every U.S. administration from Nixon to Clinton assumed it would get its way at least 95 percent of the time. But it always reserved the right to go it alone if it didn't. U.S. diplomacy was good enough that the bluff had never been called. In 2003, it was called.

Why can't the U.S. simply go back to soft multilateralism? Because once the U.S. has displayed its raw power *against its allies*, none of the three tactics are viable any more. Partnership no doubt still appeals to some governments in NATO. But the key ones have grown very wary of the U.S. And the opinions of the people in other countries that are still seeking partnership are not with their governments. Look at France. Pascal Boniface, director of the mainstream Institut de Relations Internationales et Stratégiques, writing in the principal conservative newspaper *Le Figaro*, argues that Bush merely amplified the policies of "multilateralist" Clinton, concluding: "We are not about to see normalized relations between France and the United States." And the historically pro-American François Heisbourg, of the more conservative Fondation pour la Recherche Stratégique, is scarcely friendlier: "France has been right for months. . . . [T]o think that 'old Europe' is going to jump into the same hole that the Americans are trying to get out of, that's fantasy land." In Germany, the most popular thing that Chancellor Schröder has done in recent years, during a time when he and his party have otherwise been in trouble, is standing up to the United States. And France and Germany have now announced a much closer coordination of their foreign policies, which is certainly not good news for the U.S. State Department. This coordination represents the reinforcement of the idea of a hard European core within the European Union, one that is autonomous and therefore does not need to follow the U.S. lead. The new prime minister of Spain, José Luis Rodriguez Zapatero, has announced not only that Spain will withdraw its troops from Iraq but that Spain will move to align itself with the French-German efforts to construct an independent European Union.

As for Putin, he plays a cagey game, trying not to irritate the U.S. too much. But when the chips are down, he no longer goes along with the U.S. Witness his overt move to continue to help Iran build a nuclear plant. He may cancel Iraqi debts (which he'd have a hard time collecting), but only if he gets new Iraqi contracts. And in Great Britain in 2003, George Bush visited a country where he had to be hidden from and protected against the British people. Bush didn't address Parliament because he feared being publicly heckled. Not like the good old days. Compare his trip with that of Reagan.

On all fronts, we are moving forward to a Europe that is at least as much in competition with the United States as in alliance. Partnership? Partnership against whom? In East Asia, it may be true that all four regional powers—China, Japan, South Korea, and North Korea—have reservations about one another and harbor long-standing grievances. Nevertheless, none of them is an unconditional U.S. ally, and all of them are edging toward closer relations with the other three. How close is yet to be seen, but East Asia is on the rise and is not about to take second place to a weakened United States, no matter how "multilateral" Washington claims to be.

Before September 11, many potential nuclear powers in the South were indeed hesitating. If they made a bomb, they risked U.S. (and often European) wrath. It was expensive. It wasn't all that easy to do. But now? Any country in the South that has looked at the second Iraq war can draw from it one simple lesson: Iraq was invaded not because it has weapons of mass destruction but because it didn't. All the talk about the superweapons the U.S. has been developing forces everyone to think about how they could possibly defend themselves against a United States they do not trust. One old-fashioned atomic bomb can make the U.S. hesitate seriously. That is what has become clear in the case of North Korea. For one little bomb can cause enough havoc to make it very expensive for the United States to go preemptive—expensive in terms of U.S. lives lost, and of the willingness of U.S. public opinion to tolerate such losses. And the more bombs a country of the South can amass, the better. The U.S. says it doesn't trust these countries not to use such bombs—against neighbors, against the United States. But the countries of the South think it is far more likely that the U.S. will use such bombs (at least the so-called minibombs) against them than vice versa. We don't have to debate who is right. The fact is that the countries of the South will continue to act on this assumption and are not likely to be much more accommodating to a new "multilateralist" United States than they are to George W. Bush. The Brazilian generals gave up their program in the 1980s. In Brazil, today, they are mumbling about reviving it. Yes, Libya has "renounced" making the bomb it was in fact incapable of making, lacking the necessary skilled personnel. And Iran is allowing inspections. But inspections, as we know, will not really stop the process since, under present rules, a country can do everything necessary to prepare the terrain for a bomb, then renounce the treaty and make the weapons. President Bush has called for closing this "loophole," but can he get such an amendment to the treaty adopted? Will he even bother trying? By 2015, we may expect to see another dozen nuclear powers, no matter who is president of the United States. The whole program of containing nuclear proliferation is in tatters, and trying to revive it is probably an enormous waste of energy. The U.S. has got to learn to live with it, which is quite a new situation.

Finally, globalization is just about passé. It was more or less buried at Cancún in September 2003. What happened is that the countries of the South (led by Brazil, India, China, and South Africa) called the bluff of the free traders. They said free trade works both ways. If you want the South to open up to the North, then the

North must open up to the South: No more subsidies to Northern producers, no more tariffs to keep out goods from the South. Of course, the North never really wanted that to happen. It would be political dynamite at home. So the so-called Group of 21 said, well then, bye-bye! After Cancún, the 2003 Miami meeting of the Free Trade Area of the Americas (FTAA) escaped the Cancún fiasco only because the United States and Brazil agreed to take anything important off the agenda. In short, Brazil won. The U.S. may twist the arm of El Salvador to sign a trade agreement, but what interests U.S. capitalists are the Brazilian and Argentinian markets, not that of El Salvador.

This attitude was made possible by three things. The first was the accumulation of negative effects of IMF and WTO policies in the South. Witness the economic collapse of Argentina, which had been the "good boy" of the IMF in the 1990s. The second was the stunning emergence of a worldwide "family of movements," the World Social Forum (of Porto Alegre), which, despite its very loose structure and incredible assemblage of all kinds of groups, has become a major political force in the world-system, eclipsing its rival, the World Economic Forum (of Davos). And, not least, the third was the U.S.'s continuing difficulties in Iraq, which have tied down its resources and political energy to the point that it is unable to mobilize successfully against the rising resistance to anything that has the smell of still more globalization.

Tomorrow, in a post-Bush period, if we have a "multilateralist" U.S. government, can it come to terms with the Group of 21? Can it construct an FTAA? Well, yes, provided it is ready to open U.S. (and European) frontiers to an inward flow of goods from China, India, Brazil, South Africa, and all the tiny, weaker countries of the South. But is anyone seriously contemplating this?

Bill Clinton, champion of free trade, wasn't. In any case, after George W. Bush, the price for any deal has gone up. The governments of the South will no longer be content with a little more aid and an occasional reduction of the prices of pharmaceuticals they have to buy. They want substance now, and substance means changing the structure of the world-economy in ways that reduce the advantage (and probably the standard of living) of the peoples of the North.

What can the U.S. do to get out of the deep hole into which the Bush policy has dug it? It will not be easy. One has to think of an intelligent U.S. stance vis-à-vis the world in three time dimensions: the short term going to 2010, the middle term going from 2010 to 2030, and the long term. In an electoral system, the short term commands the greatest interest of the elected officials, for remaining in power depends on the short term. But for the country, and especially for the younger generations, the middle term is more important. And for the world as a whole, the longer term is in the end the most crucial.

Let us start not with policy but with collective attitude, an issue that cuts across the time dimensions. The United States—its government but, even more so, its people—has to stop thinking of itself as the greatest country in the world and start thinking of itself as one mature country among many, one that has had both greatness and things to repent in its past, as have most of the others. Today it is a very strong country in a multipolar world that has encompassed, and will continue to encompass, other strong countries. Multipolarity is a great virtue, not a danger for the United States. To survive, or at least to survive well, the U.S. has to decide to enter into dialogue with the rest of the world. It is not that the U.S. has nothing to offer the world; it has plenty. But it has a lot to receive from the rest of the world as well. And it can only offer if it is ready to receive.

Such a change in outlook would be a socio-psychological shift of a major order, the kind that governments and peoples have great difficulty making, especially since the major political figures and the media usually find profit and comfort in purveying the opposite line. And yet, there is no real choice. For unless Americans somehow find it within themselves to make this shift, they will become ever more isolated from the rest of the world. They will find themselves not admired but besieged, and they will find it impossible to realize their own ideals.

Socio-psychological shifts of this order are not unknown in modern history. They are perhaps not even rare. But they usually occur only as a result of some dramatic occurrence—a traumatic defeat, a great victory after great effort, a profound disillusionment with leaders and ideologies in which people had rested their aspirations. The shock of September 11 might have provided the basis for such a turning point. But instead it was rapidly exploited for other ends. And the moment has passed. All we have now is the steady wearing away of the prestige, the security, and the collective wealth of the United States. And a slow but persistent downslide leads often to very bad modes of reacting. We have every reason to fear the effects of such a grating negative climate on the collective psychology of the United States.

Still, the situation is not at all hopeless. For one thing, more Americans than we might suspect by reading the world (and American) press are deeply concerned by the moral dilemmas in which the country, and its government, has placed itself. If they saw a positive program on the horizon, many would rally to it. But it has to be a program of more than the same old thing, more than a restitution of lost glory. It has to be a program of future moral and political hope, something that xenophobic nationalism tinged with racist arrogance is incapable of offering.

In the short term—that is, immediately—the United States has to reverse, 180 degrees, the three main pillars of its world strategy of the Nixon-to-Clinton years. First, it needs to accept, graciously, the political independence of Western Europe and East Asia, recognizing them as political peers that have the right to independent structures in which the U.S. has no say (such as military forces or currency policies). The U.S. would of course seek to defend its interests in its discussions with the rest of the world, but it needs to give up the idea that it should, that it can, undermine the construction of these emerging structures of its erstwhile dependent allies. And of course, the U.S. would have to accept that, to the extent there are or come to be world laws and norms, it has no right to claim any exemption whatsoever from them. Quite the contrary, the U.S. ought to be pushing for everyone to come in under the same umbrella.

Nuclear proliferation is inevitable. And it's not, as most people in the wealthy countries seem to believe, at all necessarily bad. In 1945, the U.S. was the only nuclear power. As of 2004, there are at least eight such powers and many others on the road to getting there. Going from one to eight did not lead to nuclear war, and it's not more likely that going from eight to twenty-five would do so. Indeed, one could make the case that it would actually reduce the likelihood of nuclear wars. To be sure, if the great powers could arrange very large reductions in nuclear stockpiles, this would be a plus all around. But the "middle powers" of the world, especially those in the South, are simply not going to accept having zero weapons while the U.S. has thousands. Knocking one's head against a stone wall has never been an intelligent or useful tactic. The U.S. should stop doing it. The worst of all policies—worst politically and worst morally—is to say that the existing nuclear powers may remain at, or increase, their present strength but that no one else may join them.

Neo-liberal globalization has had its day; it is now dead. In the economic turmoil of the first quarter of the twenty-first century, the major centers of capital accumulation will probably be more, not less, protectionist. And the South is not going to permit further penetration without reciprocity. In 2004, the world is coming out of, not into, a free trade era. In the 1997 financial crisis, the Asian country that did best was Malaysia, the only one that outrightly and publicly rejected the advice of the IMF. What the U.S. should be encouraging at home and abroad is the kind of economic policies that will decrease, not increase, polarization (internally in countries, and worldwide among countries). Capitalists (American and others) should return to being genuine entrepreneurs—that is, taking risks, reaping the gains if they are adept, and accepting the losses if they are not. Enterprises, in the U.S. and elsewhere, should get off their state welfare fix.

Will such a radical reversal ensure U.S. safety, health, and prosperity? There are no guarantees. But it has a far better chance than either the Bush doctrine or the now-defunct Nixon-to-Clinton policies of soft multilateralism. Above all, it would allow the U.S. to hold its head high once again, as a country that tries to live its presumed ideals and, with some difficulty (the kind everyone has), not only seeks to promote the well-being of its inhabitants but also encourages them to be good citizens of the world. The U.S. was once admired for doing this. It might be again.

Even such a radical reversal of world policy would, nonetheless, merely be the beginning. It would do no more than allow the U.S. to be a serious player, once again, in the ongoing geopolitics of the world-system, a player whose views other countries will consider worthy of taking into account and respecting. But of course, the world would be moving on, and not everything that is likely to happen would be acceptable to the American people or be helpful to their legitimate needs. We would have to assess what is likely to happen in the middle run—that is, the period 2010–2030.

First, there would likely be an important shift in geopolitical alignments. Europe would probably achieve closer integration across the continent (one that would include in some manner Russia), and it would probably have created a stronger collective military structure. It would be pursuing vigorously the accumulation of capital and technological advance. And it would be working hard to restore its cultural autonomy on the world scene. None of this would be easy to accomplish. There are important internal differences within Europe: an economic divide between its strong northwest and its economically much weaker eastern and southern segments; a second economic divide that reflects the classic left-right division (capital-labor) in European politics; among the east-central European countries, a continuing fear of or at least discomfort with Russia and, for many, even with Germany as well, albeit to a lesser extent; a reluctance of some more than others to weaken significantly the ties to the United States; and not least, all the difficulties that derive from seeking to integrate a significant and fast-growing Muslim population into the European cultural patterns. Still, Europe is likely to emerge as a major force on the world scene, and Atlanticism is likely to become a concept of the past.

What both the United States and Europe will face is an emergent East Asian complex, a third serious pole of both capital accumulation and military strength. East Asia is, and has always been, composed of three major civilizational complexes—China, Korea, and Japan—all of which have a long, continuous, and quite glorious history. Today, Korea is divided into two states, more or less equal in size. And China has what amounts to a breakaway province, Taiwan, which is itself quite divided internally about its preferred geopolitical future. Taiwan is of course far smaller than that part of China within the effective boundaries of the People's Republic of China, but it has a vigorous economy and a high level of sophistication and human capital, which give it a certain ability to pursue its own political objectives.

Both China and Korea were divided in the wake of the Soviet-American ideological conflict and so-called cold war. They were both divided as a consequence of military conflict on their soil. In some respects these are matters of the past, but despite all the ideological and political changes that have occurred in the world since 1989, such divisions remain quite deep. Nonetheless, there are strong motivations—both of nationalist sentiment and of economic self-interest—that sustain drives for reunification. It would be foolish to underestimate the strength of these drives in either Korea or China. There is probably a better than even chance of such re-unifications, under one formula or another, in the first quarter of the twenty-first century. And were the reunifications to occur, there would ensue a strong demand for some sort of economic and even possibly political integration of East Asia. Such an "East Asian union" would then come to be, by 2025, possibly the strongest node of capital accumulation in the world-system as well as a formidable military presence and a principal political actor drawing most of Southeast Asia into its orbit.

Also by 2025, we may expect that what is now a de facto economic triad—the United States, Western Europe, East Asia—would have become a political and even military triad. All talk of an American empire, or even of American world leadership, will probably have disappeared from the vocabulary of the world's media and the pontifications of the world's intellectuals. The real choice for the United States may well be whether it aligns itself with East Asia or with a Western Europe that may well have drawn Russia into its orbit. And if the United States were to find it easier and economically more profitable to be aligned with East Asia, it might well, in 2025, find itself defined as the junior partner. Furthermore, the United States might well find itself bereft of its last and most significant economic strength—its control of the world financial markets, which it currently enjoys because of the dominance of the dollar as the only reserve currency. Once that advantage disappears, and we live in a world of a triad of major currencies, the United States will begin to pay the economic price of its present self-indulgence in speculative wealth plunder and unfruitful investments in military hardware.

In this remodeled geopolitical scene of 2025, what role will be played by the countries we today call the South, and in particular by the strongest of them (strongest economically, demographically, and politically)—India, Indonesia, Iran, South Africa, Nigeria, Brazil, and Argentina, to name a few of the most obvious ones? That remains the most uncertain question. The answer depends in part on the cycles of the world-economy. If between 2010 and 2025 there is a renewed cycle of real economic growth (not stock market speculation), it is possible that part of that growth will benefit segments of the populations in these countries and also, of course, the state treasuries. And if there arises a limited political alliance among these countries as a force in international negotiations—of which the G-20 bloc's launching at the meetings of the World Trade Organization was a first serious attempt—then these countries might be able to obtain various economic concessions by playing off the members of the triad against each other. And if these countries feel wealthy enough to acquire nuclear weapons, there may be at least a dozen new nuclear powers in the South by 2025. Such nuclear capacity does not guarantee that they shall turn into military threats, but it does mean that they will be far less vulnerable to being bullied by countries in the North. On the other hand, if a significant number of their more skilled persons migrate, legally or illegally, to the North, they may thereby lose some economic leverage, although such a migratory pattern would also have the effect of aggravating the conditions of internal conflict within the North.

But all of these "ifs" are uncertain, and the degree of likelihood that these countries will follow this trajectory is at best only medium. It is probable that, as of 2025, the North-South divide in the world-system will not be significantly reduced; indeed, it might be quite enlarged. A divided North and an ever more desperate South is not a formula for pax Americana or any other version of pax.

This then brings us to the long term. The geopolitical alignments of the middle term presume, and are based on, the rules that have governed the functioning of the capitalist world-economy as an historical system. But what do we know of the trajectory of our existing world-system and the future of these rules? The outlook is not very good for the long-term survival of the capitalist world-economy. Whatever one's preferences, this statement is meant here as description of reality, not moral prescription.

The structural strains of our existing system are very great and are in the process of limiting severely the future possibilities of accumulation of capital, which has always been the central objective of capitalism as an historical system and its socio-psychological motor. There are three long-term trends that are basic to the operations of the system and are approaching the limits of their capacity to function. One is the steadily rising worldwide cost of personnel in all economic operations. The second is the steadily rising pressure on enterprises to internalize the total costs of production. And the third is the steadily rising rates of taxation at all levels of governmental structures.

Each of these structural trends is reducing the level of possible profit, and the aforementioned trio is in the process of constraining severely the ability to pursue capital accumulation at a meaningful level. Let us consider briefly what is causing these structural pressures and why they are unlikely to be more than marginally reversed.

The cost of personnel is and always has been a function of the relative political strength of capital and labor. There is no economically correct cost of labor. From the viewpoint of the employer, the lower the cost the better. From the viewpoint of the employee, the higher the recompense the better. The essential weapon of the employer is the ability to replace the current employee with one who is equally skilled but willing to accept lower recompense. The essential weapon of the employee is organization, which enables a group of employees to put political and economic pressure on the employer such that it becomes less costly for the employer to grant increased recompense than to continue to resist the demand.

Organization by employees requires a social milieu in which they can communicate with one another and in which they have learned the skills of organization, have acquired knowledge about the real alternatives of an employer, and have been able to force upon the state a relative neutrality. To achieve this combination takes time, education, and usually an urban setting. To the extent that such syndical action becomes possible and the political position of the employees in a given locale is strong enough to force the acceptance of their demands for increased recompense, employers eventually find that the value of relocation to a friendlier locale is the only tactic that can remedy this situation, once the rising costs of labor are higher than the costs of displacement and the increase in transactions costs. For five hundred years, employers have been, sporadically but repeatedly, engaged in the practice of the "runaway factory."

The runaway factory assumes that one has somewhere to run, somewhere with a weaker labor force ready to accept lower recompense for the same kind of work. What is always necessary is to find a locale that has a potential work force for whom the lower levels of recompense (lower as measured on a global scale) are in fact higher than what such workers would otherwise obtain. This is most likely to occur in locales in which there is an underemployed rural work force (preferably one not fully engaged in the money economy) who can be attracted (or constrained) to engage in such work. Such work forces have always existed, up to now. But each time such a relocation takes place, the result is a diminution of the world reserves of such available workers to attract. In the twenty-first century, worldwide deruralization has occurred to such a degree that these reserves will soon be exhausted. And this means that it will be ever more difficult to use the tactic of the runaway factory in order to reduce labor costs.

Keeping the costs of the inputs of production low has always been another primary concern of entrepreneurs. The major mechanism by which this has been done is to "externalize" as many of these costs as possible. Externalizing costs means having someone other than the entrepreneur pay for part of the costs of inputs—this someone being either the government or "society" (that is, individuals other than the producer). There are three major costs that have been externalized. One is the cost of disposal of waste, particularly toxic waste. Basically, entrepreneurs have preferred simply to dump such waste where they could. The second is the cost of renewing resources utilized in production. Entrepreneurs have preferred to be unconcerned with this problem, leaving it to future generations to worry about. The third is the cost of what is called infrastructure—the necessary large-scale foundation of transport and communications—without which no entrepreneur could obtain supplies or merchandise products.

As the world has become deruralized, so the virgin sources of basic materials and the empty areas into which one could dump waste have steadily become reduced, in some cases exhausted. The world has discovered this problem in the last fifty years, calling it the problem of ecological limits and dangers. The only long-term solution to this problem is the total internalization of such costs by the producer. But this of course squeezes profits. Similarly, the costs of infrastructure have steadily risen to the point where the demand that these costs be significantly internalized, too, has become a strong one.

Dealing with the problems of previously externalized costs requires long-term internalization but short-term state investment in clean-up and resource renewal operations. And these operations of course mean increased taxation. This, however, is not the only, not even the most important, reason for the rise in taxation rates. The fundamental explanation of the steady rise in these rates at all levels of government is the democratization of the world. That is to say, more and more people in more and more parts of the world have been demanding of their governments (and getting from them) three things—education, health costs coverage, and guarantees of lifetime income. We sometimes refer to these collectively as the welfare state. In the time since such demands were first put forward politically, in roughly the middle of the nineteenth century, their level and geographic spread have been going up steadily. And therefore, inevitably, the cost of taxation to meet these demands has been going up as well. Nothing will bring these costs down significantly because even those who complain of the high levels of taxation do not want any of their own entitlements to diminish. Quite the contrary.

The states are all caught in a squeeze between the entrepreneurial class, which sees its profit levels declining in productive activities, and the voters, who insist on higher level of recompense, further internalization of costs, and an ever-expanded welfare state. The result is relative paralysis. Nor can the states coast any longer on the implicit promise of solutions for these problems in the future. The long efforts of the historic antisystemic movements to obtain power in the states and to use this power to create a more egalitarian, less polarized social system (nationally and worldwide) reached their historic limits sometime in the 1960s. These movements, having achieved political power almost everywhere at that time, were not able to achieve the transformations they had promised. Witness the disillusionments not only with the Communist parties in power but with the social-democratic parties and national liberation movements in power. The sense that the road to transformation lay through acquiring state power was undone, resulting in a loss of faith among ordinary people in this route to social transformation.

So, we have arrived at a situation in which the entrepreneurs face an impasse in the further accumulation of capital and the popular forces have reached an impasse in transforming the world via acquiring state power. This double impasse is expressed in a chaotic world situation, with great and frequent oscillations in the economic and political arenas and a loss of cultural certainties. It is amidst this chaos that we are living today. The attacks of 9/11 and the Bush fiasco are simply reflections of this chaos, which will continue for some time. Such turmoil is a central part of the process of the collapse of an historical system. And it means that there is a real conflict not so much about the present system but about what kind of system will succeed our present one.

This fundamental conflict is, in the end, more important than the geopolitical realignments among the triad or even the North-South conflict. For whereas the end of our existing system is in process and whereas the kind of system that will replace it is absolutely uncertain, we can see two possible alternative varieties of successor systems—one that maintains the pattern of hierarchical, unequal, and polarizing structures of the present system and one that is fundamentally more democratic and more egalitarian. We can call this the battle between the spirit of Davos and the spirit of Porto Alegre.

Davos refers to the World Economic Forum's annual meetings, which, over the last twenty-five years, have occurred in the Swiss town of Davos. These meetings have brought together the elites of the world-system—politicians, entrepreneurs, the media, academics—all devoted to pursuing, under the aegis of "globalization," a program of world restructuring that would create a new world-system as hierarchical and inegalitarian as the present capitalist world-economy. And Porto Alegre refers to the annual meetings since 2001 of the World Social Forum (WSF), which took place initially in the Brazilian city of Porto Alegre. The meetings of the WSF brought together a wide variety of local, national, and international organizations, all opposed to neo-liberal globalization and imperialism in all its forms—organizations comprising laborers, women, environmentalists, indigenous peoples, and marginalized segments of the world population who share primarily their determination to achieve a more democratic and egalitarian world and are deeply suspicious of the traditional path of seeking state power as the road to transforming the world.

The forms this battle between the spirit of Davos and the spirit of Porto Alegre will take over the next twenty to thirty years are difficult to predict. But one can be sure that this is the crucial battle determining our collective future. The basic alternative to the theme of an endless war on terrorism is the theme that "another world is possible"—the slogan of the World Social Forum. This battle, however, will occur within the framework of an evolving geopolitical framework and a constant struggle between North and South. Thus a very complex scenario is created. In order to navigate this kind of global anarchy with the hope of emerging with a more sensible world structure, we have to be lucid in our understanding of the multiple loci of struggle and to be wary of the simplistic explanations that interested parties constantly furnish us in order to obscure the realities of these conflicts.

We are faced, all of us, with a very difficult and unpleasant age of transition—one dangerous for us individually and collectively, and one that on the surface is very confusing. But this is also a period of great creative possibilities, one in which we have more leeway to shape our collective futures than people normally have when the world-system in which they live is relatively stable and therefore less malleable. We need to apply ourselves intellectually, morally, and politically in order that the spirit of Porto Alegre prevails.

Index

Note: Because "United States" and "George W. Bush" appear on almost every page of this book, they are not listed in this index. To find a topic that includes either "United States" or "George W. Bush," look under the associated topic.

About the Author

Immanuel Wallerstein is a senior research scholar at Yale University and author most recently of *Decline of American Power* (New Press, 2003), *Utopistics: Or Historical Choices of the Twenty-First Century* (New Press, 1998); and *After Liberalism* (New Press, 1995).

6903 016